INDIA

BY MORTIMER MENPES
TEXT BY FLORA ANNIE
STEEL · PUBLISHED BY
ADAM & CHARLES BLACK
SOHO SQUARE · LONDON

Published November 1905

CONTENTS

CONTENTS vii

LIST OF ILLUSTRATIONS

INDIA

CHAPTER I

THE GATES OF PEARL

THE Gate of Tears lies behind us. Our faces are set eastward to the Land of the Rising Sun—to the land where sunshine is the heritage of the poorest beggar.

But we Westerns do not appreciate this heritage at its full value. We wear pith hats to keep it out of our brains, and pad the small of our back with cotton to keep it out of our marrow, and not one of us in a thousand knows the luxury of light on the bare body, unless, indeed, we have paid a guinea for a radiant heat bath, which in India one can have all day and every day free of expense.

So, as we sit, this last evening on board ship, on the forward anchor, catching the breeze of our own making, the question rises, " How far out in the Indian Ocean may we count India ? "

I knew a man once, returning reluctantly to a jungle station after a really fancy furlough, who said that he could smell the Bombay bazaar in longitude 68°; which is absurd, since, pungent as a bazaar is, even assafœtida cannot travel three hundred miles.

And yet the real edge of India does lie somewhere about there; if not in the charts, still in the map of the mind. For, look down into the water through which the black keel is slipping so oilily that the little nautilus boats take no harm, but ride away on the long smooth ripple which parts the sea, leaving place for our huge vessel. Look down, I say, and through the milky, almost opalescent depths, what are those snake-like restless brown forms seen, half seen, twining, intertwining? To the practical scientific botanical eye, it is the zone of sea-weed which, so I am told, drifts within certain limits all round India. But to the old navigators—and to the eye of faith nowadays—it is the zone of sea-serpents, the zone of sea-guardians between the outside world and enchanted India.

This is the true line dividing those who can see behind the veil, from those to whom a spade must ever be a spade, and not the unit of man's civilisation, the means by which he first forced Mother Earth to yield him—not what was to be found

ready to his sight and hand—but those things that his heart desired. For the first quest for art was the quest for bread, and through that came the knowledge that man does not live by bread alone. So, let me lay a wager, that those who looking down can see in the ever-restless motion of those brown filaments nothing but a curious natural phenomenon due possibly to the exceeding activity of infusoria, which have attached themselves to floating portions of the *Ectocarpus confervoides,* or the *Asperococcus canallenlata,* or any other of the phæosporeæan algæ, may as well turn back on the spot; for they will never see India. For them it will always remain what the botanical, scientifical, geographical, political, zoological, and, above all, sociological eye perceives it to be; that is to say, a vast country wherein almost everything exists—wherein you can at your ease study the saxifrages of the snow line and the palms of the tropics, and where you can run every idea the world has ever possessed to its bitter end, and point out with one and the same breath the advantages of patriarchal monarchy and the blessings of a National Congress. They will see the railways, and the ascetics who ride in those railways holding their third-class tickets in hands shrivelled to a claw by years of immobile penance.

They will ride in Commissioners' carriages, or
mount in the saddle—I say it advisedly—of a
stirrupless country gig.   They will inspect the
tombs of dead kings, the temples of dead gods, and
let us say, the Dufferin hospitals, and the Victoria
Memorial at Calcutta—but——

They will never find India !

On the other hand, those who can see in that
clear-obscure something which appeals to the
imagination, which tells them of hidden treasure,
of half-forgotten secrets guarded jealously from
alien eyes, may go on.   For them the gates are
open.   They will find and love India—as I do.

The evening closes in.   The opalescent sea
mingles with the opalescent sky.   There is no
horizon.   Above, below, the unseen sun sends
prismatic hues through the misty heat-sodden air
like the pearly tints on a nautilus' shell, over sea
and sky.   The world for us is blent into one perfect
Whole, All-sufficing, Indivisible.

Only that one black line, the keel of our
consciousness, disturbs it for a time with smooth
ripples which will close in behind us again to perfect
peace.

And India, guarded by its seaweed snakes, lies
ahead of us, hidden by these Gates of Pearl.   In

truth, however, even to the most imaginative Western eye much of the ultimate charm of India is always hidden by the outside garb of it, just as the real honesty of welcome or God-speed on the part of one's native friends is always obscured, somehow, by the highly scented *champak* garlands which they will insist on hanging round one's neck. It is part of the ceremony—a ceremony in which, to judge by my experience, a large proportion of Bombay must be permanently employed. It is to be seen in progress on board every arriving or departing vessel,—the eager Eastern faces, each one lavish of a longer and yet a longer garland; the self-conscious Western one, feeling itself like Bottom translated, touched by the underlying affection of the outward act, yet longing for the time when in house or cabin it can get rid of the absurd rubbish.

So the East comes always to the West laden with garlands and perfumes, quaint jewellery and tinsel, lavish of smile, full to the brim of hoary old wickednesses, ancient courtesies, and old customs.

To her they are all illusion, shadows on the surface of the Great Unthinkable, and as she salaams to the new master with both hands, her heart is elsewhere, dreaming of unity.

But we take her as we would take a London suburb, and provide her with electric trams and pure water.

And she has drunken of tanks for ages ere we were born, and has, from a sense of duty, suffocated her female children with cotton wool dipped in oil, and to this day does a thousand things at which civilisation must hold up holy hands of horror.

Yet, for all her unmentionable crimes, her innumerable deceits, she holds a secret which we of the West have forgotten, if we ever knew it.

She knows that "Time is not money, Time is naught."

There is, then, no occasion for hurry; we can take our time in India.

CHAPTER II

DOES any one really believe in our brotherhood with the Aryan? I doubt it.

He—taking the phrase as synonymous with the unit of what are called the teeming millions of India—is so extraordinarily dissimilar to all we know of ourselves, from the sole of his foot to the crown of his head, from the first thought of his mind till the last, that it is difficult indeed to pre-suppose a common origin.

Taking him as he appears first to our sight—a coolie against that chaotic background of Bombay, composed in equal parts of London and the *Arabian Nights*—the first thing we notice is that the absence of clothes makes no difference to his decency. He is as much dressed in a bit of string and a rag as an Englishman is in the Park. In fact an Englishman looks far more indecent without a collar or even without a tie than our Aryan brother does in a state of absolute nudity.

Now this is undoubtedly partly due to colour. That fine brown skin of his, so supple, so clear and uniform in tint, on which the high lights show so hard and sharp and the shadows are all velvety, is, as it were, a dress in itself; but the greater part is due to the unconsciousness which he shares with the animals, and his sense of unity with all nature. Why should he not be seen as all things are seen? And this unconsciousness goes very deep. He has not grasped half the things to which you cling as impregnable axioms; but, on the other hand, he accepts much that you leave out of life. Indeed the uncertainty as to what you may find in digging down into the mind of the Aryan brother is one of the chief charms of India. You never know what prize you may not compass therein. It is a paradise of inconsistencies wherein the lion lies down with the lamb, and the man who has with the utmost acuteness been criticising Mr. Chamberlain's fiscal policy will allow his firm belief in the transmutation of the baser metals into gold to leak out as a basis for the lightening of taxation.

Therefore one must always have a laugh ready

for the extravagances one may hear. Therefore, also, the wild inventions of native newspapers are not without their danger of being believed. India, practically, will believe anything. It has gone through so much since first those gentle Aryan shepherds came from—well! let us say the last new place whence philologists and anthropologists will allow them to have come—so many new races have arrived, so many new religions have appealed to its people, so many dynasties have arisen, reigned, and died, that in truth there is no limit to the possibility of more, no limit to the possibility of anything. No *gobe-mouche* is like the Indian fly-catcher! I remember years ago, when a certain star was seen through a certain comet's tail, a deputation of veiled women coming one clear night to ask me which particular day of the portent's stay was the one appointed for the burying alive of our late lady, Queen Victoria, who, being so good and gracious, was unable to die, and thus had to ordain her own passing into Paradise.

It was a quaint, withal a beautiful idea, which in truth I was somewhat loth to uproot from their kindly disturbed minds.

Yet without adding fancy to fact, there is enough

2

to gossip over and to spare in the annals of India. The life-history of our Aryan brother is an eventful history from the very beginning, when with his flocks and herds, his wives and children, he drifted down on India from the high uplands of Asia—the roof of the world.   There is in India now a tract of sandy desert—watered into fruitfulness by deep wells which dip down, so the natives say, into the waters of the lost Sarsuti River—where some of these hordes of shepherds settled, and rooting into the sand, have practically withstood the ages. There to this day they sing some of the Vedic hymns, and in half a hundred ways show themselves a remnant of the true Aryan race.   These Sarsuti, or Saraswati Brahmins, are a fine, upstanding, fair race, of high features, tall and strong, but not martial, who live by agriculture, and spend the long Indian day in watering their crops—mustard and wheat and gram in the cold weather, millet and maize in the hot—watering them from the sacred hidden river of the Goddess of Speech. For Saraswati is the Indian Pallas Athene, the wise, chaste goddess in whose honour, however, the nuptial hymn is sung :—

> Charming Sar'suti, as swift as a mare,
> Guard thou the duty which world-wide I swear.

Thy womb, Sar'suti, the universe framed,
Wisdom and beauty from thy name are named.
So to thy glory the bride sings her hymn,
Highest in story which age cannot dim,
Marriage is duty—'tis womanhood's vow;
Charming Sar'suti, be thou with us now.

So with cymbals and horns they bring the red-garmented, tearful, yet willing bride home through the green wheat-fields on some auspicious day, and the bridegroom lifts her over the milk-besprinkled, sugar-cake-decked threshold, and one more family, moulded on the old Aryan type, starts on its way rejoicing, to keep up the numbers of the old village community.

For that is one of the most ancient things in India. Learned books have been written on it, people have travelled out to India to study it, and still the secret of its cohesion, despite the disintegrating influences amidst which it stands, remains as much a mystery as ever—as much a mystery as the self-forgetting, self-sacrificing cosmogony of a hive of bees.

I am told it is beginning to yield to our Western gospel of personal comfort, but even now it remains as the thing best worth seeing in India. The individual taste of the globe-trotter may take him to Imperial durbars, to the palaces and tombs of dead kings, to the rock-cut temple-shells of dead religions; but unless he has seen a village community at work, and grasped its absolute isolation from the rest of God's world, he has not seen India.

Only one thing it cannot provide for itself: it cannot provide the mothers for its sons. For those it must go elsewhere, sending its daughters in exchange; since marriage is no question of personal liking or disliking, no question even of spiritual affinities, mutual companionship, monetary convenience, jolly chumship, or any of the thousand and one reasons for our modern matrimony, to the Aryan brother. It is simply a question of race—its purity, its preservation. The whole system of caste is in truth nothing but a complicated "table of affinities," which with us forbids a man to marry his deceased wife's sister, but with the Indian limits him to forbearance with many men's sisters.

It is an interesting subject, this one of caste; the most interesting thing about it being that caste is not an Indian but a Portuguese word.

Its Indian equivalent is *varna* or colour. This word is used throughout all the ancient literature in discrimination of the Aryas, the white people, the people of God, from the Dasyias, the black people, the aborigines or children of the Devil.

Caste, then, seems due to that hatred of miscegenation which is so marked a feature in all white races. It is a curious fact that anthropometry, which follows the track of race like a sleuth-hound, supports this view. Those castes which show clearly the characteristics of the aboriginal type are still the lowest in the social scale.

Broadly speaking, a man's social status varies in inverse ratio to the width of his nose. " Follow your nose" therefore has its justification indeed.

Missionaries, of course, hold as a rule that caste —which they designate as "the curse of India"— has a purely religious origin. To them Brahminism is the owl, caste the egg; that is to say, a natural product of a false religion.

But, curiously enough, the whole weight of real religious feeling in India is against caste. Every reformer has denounced it, many have openly rebelled against it, and pointed to that Sanskrit version of "What God has created call thou not common or unclean" which is to be found in their oldest sacred book: "There is no distinction of caste with Brahm. The whole world is Brahminical."

What is more, even in these days the true ascetic outgrows caste, as he is supposed to outgrow the sins which necessitate it.

I remember in the hill state of Chumba a very high-caste Brahmin bearer bringing me an egg in his hand; a thing which I should have deemed fatal to his pretensions to purity. He laughed. The Rajah himself was not in a position to question *his* position: that lay between him and his God.

So, underlying all the trivial distinctions of petty castes which in India seem so foolish, so degrading, stands this magnificent idea of a man standing alone before his Creator, accountable only to Him for any contamination.

There is, of course, another factor in caste besides the pride of race. It is an industrial precaution, and in the past has in India played the part of our trades guilds of the Middle Ages.

And it has such a quaint influence on the whole land from the Himalaya to Cape Cormorin that surely none can carry away with him the least grip on India without understanding something of its hereditary trades.

So let us revert to the village community where these hereditary trades linger, not altogether, yet still partially undisturbed by Manchester and Birmingham.

The potter, the carpenter, the cobbler, the

weaver, the smith—these are all the trades, if we except the undertaker, who is also the scavenger.

With artisans ready to give pots, to make shoes, to weave cloth, to forge metals, to hew wood, the village community exists independent of all save itself.

It was the one political and social organisation of buried India, and it remains so to an extent which makes much of the domestic life of the village a sealed book to outsiders. Its affairs are conducted by a council of five elders. The head man, who succeeds to the office by hereditary right, is responsible to the State for the land tax. It has its own officials, accountant, watchman, priest, musician, doctor; its own hereditary tradesmen.

In the old days from one end of the village street to the other, in house and workshop, nothing was to be found save village manufactures. Now it is otherwise, and, even in the most remote, Birmingham and Berlin is writ clear on many things exposed for sale, paraffin is burnt everywhere, and the peasant going to his fields lights his *hukka* with matches. Still the old hereditary trades survive. Perhaps the most interesting, certainly the most typical one, is that of the potter.

There he sits, on the outskirts of the village among the sherds, as his fathers, unto Heaven knows how many generations, have sate. Ask him his origin, he will reply suavely, "My father's fathers made pots for the Court of Indra (*i.e.* in Paradise), since when we have always made pots." And the droning hum of his wheel will go on evenly, the dome of clay upon it rise into a curving swan-like neck, then settle down dizzily into a globe, and so by myriads of faint, imperceptible flexions of the potter's thumb take some form consecrated by immemorial custom for the use of man; since in the village you dare not even *ask* for a new shape. As pots were in the beginning, so they are now. As we made them in Paradise, so we make them now.

Pots in Paradise!

The very words bring a sense of rest, and there are no butchers or bakers or candlestick-makers in the family to mar the even tenor of that refrain.

"We made pots in Paradise."

Above the potter the sky darkens and lightens with day or night; below him the plastic clay awaits its strange immutability of form; the pitcher breaks, but another and yet another goes to the well.

Though the clay be base and the potter mean,
The pot brings water to make souls clean,

says the old rhyme.   So, even a high-caste Hindu
may drink from a vessel that comes straight from
the potter's kiln, alight though that be with the
refuse of the village; but he must break it after
the drink—that is the ritual of the pot.   Again,
when either birth or death touches a Hindu household, every pot in it must be broken and a new
one put in its place.   Possibly a bald fear of defile-
ment may partially dictate this custom; but in
addition there is undoubtedly the esoteric teaching
that all life, both that which comes and that
which goes, needs to begin anew.

Now it is this suggestiveness in his daily life,
this unceasing iteration that about him there lies,
as it were, a fourth dimension before which our
three-dimensioned space becomes illusive, which
differentiates our Aryan brother from his fellow-
worker in the West, whose view of life is, alas!
so often bounded on all sides by the ultimate
sixpence.

And it is this suggestiveness which is the true
Indian local colour lurking alike in shadow and
shine.   The picture may be vivid enough: we
may see the varied life of the bazaars, the quiet of

3

the fields, the vice of the towns, the unalterable obstinacy and patience of the people, even the spurious civilisation of such centres as Calcutta and Bombay ; but without this atmosphere we do not see the true India.

It is like that dusty background of the Northern Provinces—that wonderful biscuit-coloured background which softens yet strengthens every tint which touches it.

So the Bombay coolie almost naked, certainly extortionate, has yet to be reckoned with as the most noticeable factor in picturesque India.

CHAPTER III

ITS BURIED HISTORY

INDIAN history, treated as history, is a **Dead Sea fruit.** One is left with the ashes of dead dynasties in the mouth. Yet viewed as a romance it is full to the brim of almost magical charm; not least that portion of it which may be termed its buried history—the history which lies buried among the ruins around Delhi or Indrapasthra, at Ayodhya, at Hastinipur, and deeper still in some of those as yet unexplored mounds in the wide plains of the north-west which local tradition points out as the site of an ancient city. Some of these are so little raised above the surrounding levels that one needs to see them against a sunset sky before the faint curve asserts itself. But when once seen the memory of it never fades. The glow of a dying day behind a slight mound of shadow—that is all which remains of the palaces and fortresses of the

19

old Serpent race which, ages before the Aryans set
foot in India, had wrested a part of the land, at
any rate, from the original owners, the Kols, and
the Bhils, and other aboriginal tribes. Who these
Nagas were, it is impossible to say. Our only
record of them beyond acres of huge bricks, which
in the Punjab are to be found in many places
under the sand-hills, are the allusions to them in
the two great Hindu epics, the Mahabarata and
the Ramayana. But they still rule India, for
deep down in the hearts of the people lies the
worship of the snake. That has never been
forgotten, and still throughout the length and
breadth of India, the childless wife creeps out to
some snake's hole with her offering of milk and
sugar, and the cobra lives secure in its sanctity;
for a native rarely kills one except under dire
distress. He would rather salaam to it, and let it
slip unharmed on its way. On a certain day in
August nearly all India worships the snake with
laughter and jollity, the women amusing themselves by making counterfeit presentments of the
coiled creatures and frightening their men folk
with them, while in the evening those people
who still claim to be of the Snake tribe have
the privilege of carrying the images round on

winnowing baskets and collecting gifts for the snake.

That, in the beginning, these Nagabansis or Takkas were a kingless republican race we know; also that they were very rich and very luxurious, famous for their beautiful women and exhaustless treasures. Such fragments of history or legend regarding them as linger to these days are all extraordinarily stimulating to the imagination; and even the records of their later days, when the republicanism had been forgotten, and Naga king fought with Naga king, and when the great Chandragupta ruled at Paliputra, the present Patna, and also at Takkashila in the Western Punjab, are full of fire and romance.

The history of Asoka alone would make the Naga race remarkable. Grandson of Chandragupta, he began his reign with the nickname of "The Furious," and ended it after three and thirty years as Piyadarsi, "The Loving-minded,"—a great change for an Eastern monarch who commenced by killing all his brothers after the fashion of those days. Nor was the change to be attributed to his conversion to Buddhism, for the four years of his greatest fury followed on his adhesion to that religion.

Whether it is true that in after years he came under the influence of Jainism, that most tender-hearted of faiths, I know not, but certainly the edicts which remain to this day scattered over India, on rock and pillar, point to some teaching higher even than that of Sakymuni. They are well worth reading, these pronouncements of the old Naga-Maurya king who lived in the third century before Christ,—not the least remarkable one of them being that which ordains medical aid to all his people, even the "birds of the air and the beasts of the field."

None of our Governments, neither Conservative nor Liberal, have found time even to suggest such a measure. Neither have we as a nation learnt to include in the catalogue of things for the welfare of which each one of us, as citizen, is responsible, the lives and rights of our fellow-mortals, the beasts that perish. So let every one who visits India take note with tears of at least one of the Griefless (a literal translation of Asoka) King's edicts. There are two at Delhi.

But before Asoka's day a very momentous event had occurred. Alexander of Macedon had led a Greek phalanx into the land of the Five Rivers, and though his army refused to cross the

Sutlej and he had eventually to return whence he came, he had left an indelible mark on India. To this day the Yunani or Greek system of medicine is practised by the Indian hakims, and just as, along the line of march of Alexander's army, coins, statues, bas-reliefs turn up in the sandy soil which are absolutely Grecian in feeling, so even now there are traces of the dead conqueror in the lives of the people. Chandragupta, it is true, drove the Greeks out of India—after having married a Greek princess,—but even he could not end their influence; for long centuries after his death a monarch reigned in his stead, whose name was Sotor Megas—the Nameless King—and whose coins bear the legend—

ΒΑΣΙΛΕΩΣ ΒΑΣΙΛΕΩΝ

A mysterious, dream-compelling personality is this of the unknown Bactrian "King of Kings," whom some claim to have been King Azes, others Vikramaditya. The latter, whose date is about that of the Christian era, is the hero demi-god of Indian legend. His exploits and those of Saliva-hana, who reigned about a century later, are on the lips of half India. The very children babble of him in their fairy stories.

Praise be to Vikra majit,
He gave us pearls to eat,

say the captured wild swans in the Aryan
version of the world-wide tale. And then the
rival monarch gives them seed pearls. But one
day a pierced pearl is found in their food, and
after many adventures they make their way back
to the great Mansarobar Lake in Central Asia,
where all wild swans dwell.

Taken as the centre round which folk-tales
gather, nevertheless, Raja Rasâlu, the son of
Salivahana, stands pre-eminent. How he killed
the giants, how he became a Yogi, how he swung
the seventy maidens, how he played chess—are
not all these told again and again between darkness
and dawn, when the drone of the story-teller serves
at once as rousing stimulant and drowsy narcotic ?

There is one other personality belonging to this
period of almost buried history which has always
had and always will have overwhelming influence in
India, whether it be the India of yesterday, to-day,
or to-morrow ; for Sakyamuni or Gautema Buddha
was born at Kapila-vastu, in the sixth century
before Christ. So much has been written of him
that the bare fact of his birth and death is sufficient
here. Born of that Shesh-nag or Serpent race of

kings whom Chandragupta afterwards overthrew, he forsook his crown to sit under the Bo-tree and become a teacher, his last words, as he once again called his disciples round him, being :

"Beloved! That which causes life causes also decay and death!"

They are words which have not been forgotten in India, and never will be forgotten. For the rest, one curious little fact, not so well known as it might be, may be mentioned. Sakya has been canonised a Saint in the Roman Catholic Church under the name of St. Josaphet.

So this buried history of the centuries before our era survives in a thousand ways amongst even the ignorant peasants; and the old bardic songs, mere strings of names as many appear to us, never fail to rouse nods of interest and approval. The doings of Sikundar (Alexander) are still in the mouths of all, and until our Western education of the last thirty-five years left no time for such simple arts, every child took a pride in having at least a few stories to tell, learnt accurately from some teacher. And they are fine, blood-curdling stories those gleaned from the Ramayana and the Mahabarata. Even the marriage of the delicious Draupadi to the whole five brothers *at once*, over

4

which some historians find it "necessary to draw
a veil" (the veil it is to be presumed of modern
decency over ancient depravity—or the converse !),
is forgotten in the picture of her Swayamvara or
Maiden's-choice, when with the nuptial garland in
her hand she stood watching her suitors draw their
bows.   One, successful in hitting the mark, she
dismisses as of too mean a birth; but when Arjuna,
disguised as a simple Brahman disciple, comes for
her choice, lo ! the garland is round his young neck
in a moment.

What, too, can be finer than the gambling scene
in the tent, when with loaded dice Sakuni and the
Kaurava conspirators play with Draupadi's husband,
whom they have inflamed with wine until he wagers
and loses all—crown, kingdom, riches, liberty ; then
sets his wife on the die and loses yet once again !

So to them in the tent comes Draupadi, sent
for by her despairing husband . . . and swiftly
routs them all ! She is a free woman ; no slave
dare barter her, and was not he a slave deprived of
crown, kingdom, riches, liberty, ere he had staked
her on the throw ?

So the five brothers, rich only in Draupadi,
wander forth to the jungle and the great war of
the Pandava's for the recovery of kingship begins.

One hears the tale at night round many a village fire—ay! and many a stalwart henpecked man, so-called head of a household of women, takes comfort in the thought that even in the old golden days the grey mare was the better horse—as she is now!

And there are thousands of such stories which have been preserved wholesale by the bards, who nowadays live as they best can, wandering about within a smaller or larger area, and taking gifts for their songs. But in ancient days they had a more assured existence, and were attached to the court of every petty feudal chief. Among the Rajputs, indeed, the Charan or court herald was considered more sacred than the Brahman, and this being so, he was often used as a guardian both of honour and wealth. If, for instance, a caravan laden with bullion was waylaid by robbers, the Charan in charge would step forward waving his long white robes and calling down vengeance on all who should molest him or his. And if this were not sufficient he would stab himself, so bringing the most damnable bloodguiltiness on his enemies.

Thus, in honour also, a king's Charan staked his life on his master's word, and if insult were offered to the crown, avenged it instantly by killing—not the offenders!—but himself, in full belief that his death would cause the ruin of his master's detractors.

To this day a similar form of intimidation exists in a much modified form in out-of-the-way villages. There one of two disputants will hire a Brahman to sit on the other's doorstep without food or drink until justice be done. As the Brahman's death from starvation would entail horrible consequences in the future world, this course generally brings about a compromise, especially if a retaliatory Brahman be sent to the other disputant's door.

This system of "dharna" has, however, been made illegal by us, and in old days it certainly must have been a powerful thumbscrew, since the procedure then was slightly different. Then the Brahman appeared with poison or dagger, prepared to die if any one crossed the doorstep. Thus both within and without lay starvation, unless a settlement was brought about. Still it saved court fees, lawyers, and a variety of equally useless expense; besides, do we not still put our juries into "dharna"? and does not our House of Commons use hunger as a weapon?

But these survivals of the old buried history of India are bound to sink deeper and deeper out of

A NATIVE BULLOCK-CART, JEYPORE

sight. They will crop up here and there, like the old bricks beneath the sand-hills, to amuse antiquarians and folk-lorists. Then they will finally disappear before a bailiff's summons to attend the County Court.

Already the authority of the old village Panchiyat, "the Council of Five Elders," has almost gone. It still looks after the minor morals of the community; but even here the younger men and maidens —or perhaps one should say widows, since they practically are the only offenders—begin to question its right to parental despotism; for India seems inclined to swallow the West *en bloc*—foundling hospitals, workhouses, pauperisation, and trades unions.

In a dozen more years the buried history of Hindostan will hold many things worthy a longer life.

CHAPTER IV

FROM time immemorial the level plains of the Punjab have been the battlefield of India. Here, from some remote Central Asian cradle, the Naga-bansis settled first, gradually extending their empire to Central India, where the town of Nagpore still remains witness to their presence. Here the Aryans came, and here still the most typical colony of their race remains. Here also Alexander marshalled his hosts, and the Scyths, Bactrians, the White Huns, the Getæ (who still survive as the Jâts) marched and countermarched.

Out of this welter of races the Rajputs arose, bringing with them a romance, a chivalry almost unequalled in the world. During the early centuries of our era they were in the zenith of their power; their rule extended far down the Ganges, and it was not till the twelfth century that the

Mahommedans succeeded in driving them back westward to what still remains Rajputana. During these long centuries the whole of India seems to have been one vast battlefield, petty chief warring with petty chief; and yet all the while the war was really between the claims of these born soldiers, the Rajputs, and the claims of those born priests, the Brahmans.

The old Aryan household, in which the householder was spiritual as well as temporal head, had passed away, an earlier Brahmanism based on purely philosophical and esoteric principles confined to the intellectual few had given place to Buddhism, and now on the ashes of that faith a new Brahmanism had arisen, claiming not only spiritual but temporal power through hard and fast ritual and ceremonial binding on all; the right performance of which, however, lay entirely in the hands of the hereditary priesthood. Hence the dispute for actual supremacy.

The history of the Rajputs is a magnificent history. It links the buried India with the India of to-day, for just as they faced and fought the old kings of Magadha, half-Aryan, half-Nagabansi, so they fought the Mahommedans, so they fought us.

These sons of princes or rajahs claim to have sprung from the sun or from the moon. The former claims three races, the latter but one. There is, however, a third race, the "fire-born." This, which contains many of the most noted tribes, asserts that it was created by the gods from a fire sacrifice on Mount Abu, in order to aid the Brahmans.

In the present day Udaipore holds the headship of all Rajputs. Its ruler is descended from the sun-born kings of Ayodhya or Oude, and the golden sun, rayed on a huge disc of black ostrich feathers, is his royal insignia, to which every Hindu does homage. Rama (the great god Ram) is his ancestor; he is lineal descendant of the old Ranas of Chittore, that stronghold of Rajput chivalry— Chittore whose every stone has a remembrance.

It is to the Mahabarata and the Ramayana that we must look for the earliest history—if history it may be called—of the Rajputs; and yet to this day the race is so curiously similar to the heroes of those ancient epics that legend grows to reality as we read. There is no better description of the modern Rajput than that given by Talboys Wheeler:

"They form a military aristocracy of the feudal type. They are brave and chivalrous, keenly sensitive of an affront, and especially jealous of the honour of their women.

" Their chiefs, if occasion serve, are still prepared to lead the life of outlaws, like the five brothers, or to go into exile with the silent haughtiness of Rama. Indeed, but for the paramount power of the British Government, they would still carry on bloody feuds for generations, or engage in deadly wars which could only end in mutual extermination."

Colonel Tod also tells us that the "poorest Rajpoot retains all his pride of ancestry, often his sole inheritance; he scorns to hold the plough, or use his lance but on horseback."

The history of such a people must needs be a long tissue of tales, each one of which would form the plot of a modern novel of adventure. There is the story of Bappa Rawul, herd-boy, knight-errant, king, who brought his island princess to Udaipur, and built for her that island on the lake where she might worship—as she had worshipped in her father's house — the Great Mother who became the tutelary goddess of Mewar. The story, too, of Rao Tunno's great charge from his besieged fortress; of Deo Râj the boy bridegroom, refugee from his own fatal wedding-feast, who found the Yogi's phial containing the precious golden elixir and used it to regain his lost kingdom on condition that he wore the Yogi's dress—which the suzerain

5

princes of Jassulmer do to this hour on the day of their enthronement.

But the greatest stories of all are those connected with the three sacks of Chitore, those terrible days which make the oath "by the sin of the sack of Chitore" unalterable to a Rajput.

The first of these was brought about by the fame of Princess Padmani, whose name still survives in common parlance as the synonym for fair and virtuous womanhood.

Her renown as the greatest beauty of her day had attracted the Mahommedan conqueror Allah-u-din, and he forced his way to the bare rock of Chitore demanding to see her face, if it were only her face reflected in a mirror.

He saw it, honourably entertained by Prince Bhimsi. But the sight inflamed his desire still more, and escorted as honourably back to his camp, he seized the Prince as a ransom for the Princess.

The Chiefs of Chitore, aghast at the loss of their King, decided that Padmani must do her duty. So seven hundred litters containing the Princess and her attendants set out mournfully to the Mahommedan's camp. The husband saw his wife for one brief farewell, and then—then by Padmani's wit, from out those seven hundred litters leapt seven

hundred armed men, while each of the bearers, throwing off his slight disguise, showed armed to the teeth. With such a bodyguard Bhimsi and Padmani had time to mount fleet horses and escape.

But at a bitter cost. Surrounded by the Mahommedan army, the flower of Chitore died hard—but died.

There is scarcely anything finer in the annals of India than the story of the Rajput wife and widow who, standing beside the flaming pyre, cried to the boy who had borne himself in battle beside her dead lord:

"Tell me ere I go hence, how my lord bore himself?"

"Reaper of the harvest of battle! On the bed of honour he has spread a carpet of the slain; a barbarian prince his pillow, he sleeps ringed about by his enemies!"

"Tell me yet once again, O boy! how my love bore himself?"

"O mother! how can the world tell of his deeds! There were none left to fear or to praise him."

Years passed, and Allah-u-din, who had never forgotten the trick, returned. The maiden city was held to be impregnable, but the gold which he paid for every basketful of earth soon raised a commanding point whence he could pour his missiles into the city.

So the weary, hot days sped on slowly, until one night King Bhimsi woke in fear. In a lurid light the tutelary goddess of Chitore stood before him, saying:

"If my altar and your throne is to be kept, let twelve who wear the diadem die for Chitore."

Now Bhimsi and Padmani had twelve sons.

So one by one, in obedience to the goddess's orders, the young Princes were set on the throne. For three days they were King, and then they went forth to meet the foe and to meet fate.

Only Ajeysi remained, the darling of his father's heart.

Then Bhimsi called the chiefs together. "This shall not be," he said. "The child shall go free to recover what is lost; I will die for Chitore."

"Yea! we will die for Chitore," echoed the chieftains solemnly. "In saffron robes and bridal coronets we will die for Chitore."

Then throughout the whole city stern resolve took shape in bridal garments and a funeral pyre, vast, mysterious, set in the vaults and caverns which stretch far away into the earth.

Thither in solemn procession came the Rajput women singing, in their holiday garments, covered with their jewels.

Then, when the gate had closed upon the last woman—on Padmani—the men's turn had come! Surrounding Prince Ajeysi with a picked band of desperate warriors sworn to see the lad safe, they flung open the gates, and bridal-coroneted, saffron-robed, sought the embrace of death.

When the conqueror led his victorious troops into Chitore all was still. Only a wisp or two of thin smoke escaping from the vaults below hung earthwards or drifted skywards.

None have entered the vaults since, save one, led thither by God; and to-day the very entrance to them is forgotten, though the "sin of the sack of Chitore" still echoes from Rajput mouth to Rajput mouth.

The second sack of Chitore was in the time of Humayun, second of the three Great Moghuls; and once again a woman tried to save the city. There is an ancient custom in India, not, as some have asserted, by any means confined to the Rajputs, by which a woman may choose what is called a bracelet-brother for her defence by sending to any man—emperor or slave—a silken bracelet called a *ram-rukki*. It is made in remembrance of the bracelet which Ram's mother, Kansâlya, fastened on her son's wrist ere he started on his exile, and is a mere cord of silk bounden with tinsel, fastened with a loop and button, and hung with seven tiny little floss silk tassels, red, orange, yellow, green, blue, indigo, violet—the colours of the spectrum.

It is optional to receive it, but once bound about the wrist, and the small breast bodice which custom has chosen as the fitting return sent to the giver, the twain are brother and sister indissolubly, and from that moment he is bound to her service. He is her "dear and reverend brother," she his "dear and virtuous sister."

Now Kurnavati, mother to the baby King, saving herself from her husband's funeral fire for the child's sake, sent such a bracelet to the Emperor Humayun. "Tell him," she said to her messengers, "he is bracelet-bound brother to the Rani Kurnavati of Chitore, and that she is hard pressed by Bahadur Shah."

Humayun's every instinct was charmed with the chivalrous incident. Veritable knight-errant, full of enthusiasm, he left the conquest of Bengal on which he was engaged and hurried north. He came too late, however, and the doomed garrison prepared to die as they had died once before. Thirteen thousand women were led to a funeral pyre by the Rani herself, after she had succeeded in smuggling the infant King beyond the walls. Then what had happened before happened again. The gates were flung wide, and the remaining handful of the garrison, clad in bridal robes and

coroneted with the bridal crown, rushed, dealing
death, upon death.

Thirty-two thousand men perished during this
second siege.

Before passing to the third siege, the fate of
little Udai Singh, the baby King, deserves some
few words.

Given an asylum by his half-brother Bikramajit,
he lived in the palace with his foster-mother
Punnia. One night, when he had fallen asleep,
screams rose from the women's apartments, and
then the death wail. Accustomed to the life of
palaces, Punnia's quick brain leapt to the truth.
Conspirators had slain Bikramajit, and the next
victim would surely be Udai Singh.

To catch the child up, thrust some sugared
opium into his mouth, hide him still sleeping in a
fruit-basket, and give that into the hands of a
faithful servant, saying, "Go!—to the river-bed
without the city—wait for me," was but an instant's
quick work.

The next was not so easy,—to throw a rich
robe over her own sleeping child and wait, wait
breathlessly.

It came all too soon that question, "The Prince ?
Where is the Prince ?"

With a supreme effort she pointed to the sleeping child.

When all was over, when she had wept her full, poor soul, and the funeral rites of the supposed young King had been duly performed, she hid her face in her veil, and stern, dry-eyed, resolved, made for the river-bed. There she found her nursling, and rested not at all till, through wild hill and dale, by precipices and peaks, she reached the fortress of Komulmer.

" Guard the life of the King," she cried to Aeysha Shah, the governor, and set the child upon his knee.

It is a fine story whether it be true or untrue, and it is one that the women of India often tell.

To return to the third sack of Chitore. This happened in the days of Akbar, son of Humayun, and greatest of the Great Moghuls. It was the third and last, for the conqueror was of right royal stuff, and knew how to treat brave men. So when the final consummation was once more reached, and thousands of brave men had gone to death by the sword, and thousands of braver women met death by fire, he left the city, levying no ransom, and on the place where his camp had stood raised a white marble tower, from whose top a light might shine to cheer the darkness of Chitore.

But a few years afterwards, when in dire distress and riding for his life through an ambush, the man on Akbar's right hand and the man on his left, shielding him from blows, making their swords his shelter, were two of the defeated Rajput generals.

So much for the instinct of one born to lead men.

There is one more Rajput story, a simple little story, which yet lingers in the mind as one looks out on the lake at Udaipore — the story of the Princess Kishna Komari, the flower of Rajasthan. Fifteen years of age, lovely, lovable, she became the apple of discord between Sindhia, Juggut Singh of Ambar, and Rajah Maun of Marwar.

Distracted by fear lest one or all of these importunate suitors should sack town and palace, her father condemned her to die. She took the poison offered her, smiling, saying to her weeping mother, "Why grieve? A Rajput maiden often enters the world but to be sent from it. Rather thank my father for giving you me till to-day." This happened late in the eighteenth century, but a few years before India practically passed into the hands of the English.

So the fire and the romance, the chivalry and courage of the Rajputs have yet to be reckoned with in our treatment of India. Not so long ago—riding over one of the level sand-stretches set here and there with cane brakes and great tiger grass and patches of green crops, which in Rajputana lie between those rocky hills that grow so blue, so ethereal, seen even at a short distance—I was talking to some Thakoors of the trend of politics in India, averring that the time would soon come when the whole land would be left to the babu. One of them turned his keen high face, with its eagle eyes, from the distracting trail of pig in the jungle, and answered with an indifferent laugh : "Give me a following of twelve, and the babu's tenor of office would be short in Rajasthan."

And so it would be.

CHAPTER V

THE Rajput period overlaps the Moghul just as the buried life of India showed for a time on that welter of creed and race which followed the beginning of our era.

Mahmud of Ghuzni, Allah-u-din, and many another Mahommedan invader came into conflict with the Rajput cavalry, but it was not till Babar (first of the greatest trio of kings, following father to son, who ever existed) invaded India that the Mahommedan empire came to stay.

Now these three—Babar, his son Humayun, his grandson Akbar—are such overwhelming personalities that one is tempted to leave out of the list of the Great Moghuls those minor ones of Babar's great-grandson Jehangir and his son Shah Jehan, his grandson Aurungzebe. Yet these in ordinary company would stand out renowned. In fact, this double trio forms one of the greatest dynasties of the world.

Of Babar himself it is difficult to say enough without rousing incredulity. Poet, painter, musician, astronomer, soldier, lover, knight-errant, king, *bon-vivant*, he was all of these to perfection, and his kindly, valorous, intensely imaginative, and yet human atmosphere shows out, even after all these years, to an absolutely marvellous degree, as one reads the history of his time; still more when we take up that incomparable book, his Memoirs. He was, in fact, all things, except what he is called, a Moghul.

Of them he writes :

> If the Moghul race had an angel's birth,
> 'Twould still be made of the basest earth.
> Write the Moghul's name on thrice-fired gold,
> 'Twill ring as false as it did of old.
> From a Moghul's harvest sow never a seed,
> For the seed of a Moghul is false indeed!

A Moghul or Mongul in the East in those days being what a Tartar was in the West; that is to say, a wild wanderer, unpleasant at close quarters, and therefore best not caught !

The first entry in Babar's Memoirs runs thus:

" In the year 1494, and the twelfth of my age, I became King of Ferghana."

HUMAYUN'S TOMB

Practically he was but eleven, as he was born on St. Valentine's Day 1488.

A great many kings have perchance begun kingship earlier, but there has been some one behind the boyish hand gripping the reins of government. Babar — his real name was Zahir-ud-din, but he was nicknamed " the Tiger " as a child— held them himself from the beginning.

His description of the kingdom he came to rule gives at once his literary skill :—" Ferghana is situate on the extreme boundary of the habitable world. It is a valley clipped by snowy mountains save on the west, whither the river flows. Of small extent, it abounds in grain and fruits. Its melons are excellent and plentiful. There are no better pears in the world. Its pheasants are so fat that four persons may dine on one and not finish it. Its violets are particularly elegant, and it abounds in streams of running water. In the spring its tulips and roses blow in rich profusion, and there are mines of turquoises in its mountains, while in the valley the people weave velvet of a crimson colour."

This is the work of a heaven-born artist. As he writes, the hidden turquoise in the hills, the webs of crimson velvet, the roses, the tulips, leap to his mind's eye. The memory of many a ripe melon,

luscious pear, fat pheasant, returns to him, and the
sweet scent of the violets, the sound of the running
water, the sight of the distant snows in sunset all
combine to fill his soul with content at the beauty
he has seen.

He has this unerring touch in everything, and
his description of his father can, indeed, hardly be
matched as portraiture :

"He was of low stature, wore a short bushy
beard, and was fat ; he used to wear his tunic very
tight, and as he drew himself in when he put it on,
when he let himself out the strings often burst ;
he also wore his turban without folds, and let the
ends hang down.   His generosity was large, and so
was his whole nature ; and though he was but a
middling shot with a bow, he had such uncommon
force with his fists that he never hit a man but he
knocked him down.   He was humane—and played
a great deal at backgammon."

There is the very man before us !   And so it is
in all Babar's word-pictures.   Of his knight-errantry
there is enough and to spare in his Memoirs.   As
conqueror of Samarkand, as refugee in the mountains, as invader of India, as lover, husband, father, he
stands out above the ruck absolutely informed with
chivalry and fire.   When he was three and twenty

he attempted to cross the Koh-i-baba hills in winter.
"I have scarcely," he writes, "undergone more
hardship." It was no time to employ authority; at
such times every one who has spirit does his best,
and those who have none are not worth speaking
about. So I and my nobles ourselves worked to
trample down a path in the snow, till we could drag
our horses forward a pace or two. So for a week
we worked till we reached the pass. Here the
storm of wind was dreadful, the snow fell continu-
ously; we all expected to meet death together.

While yet light we came on a sort of small cave.
Some were for my going into it, but I felt that for
me to be in comparative comfort while my good
soldiers were in snow and drift would be in-
consistent with that fellowship in suffering which
was their due. So I dug a hole in the drift at its
mouth and found a shelter from the wind in it; by
bedtime prayers four inches of snow had settled on
me. That night I caught a cold in my ear!"

A day or two afterwards he records the fact of
having seen "thirty-two different kinds of tulips,
one yellow, and scented like a rose." Again, when
eating burnt cakes in a headsman's house during
one of his reverses, he thinks regretfully "of a
certain way they had in Ferghana of stuffing

apricots with almonds." For months on months
his mother had the only tent in his flying camp ; as
King he helped to carry her shoulder-high to her
grave, and after long years of separation from his
wife, he simply writes, "It was Sunday at mid-
night when I met Maham again " : Maham—mother
of Humayun and his sisters Rose-face, Rose-form,
Rose-blush—being practically his only wife.

This then was the paladin who appeared victorious
on the arid plains of India, and found its luxury
Dead Sea fruit before the sight of "an apple tree in
full blossom," or the autumn leaves in his far-away
hills, "which no painter however skilful could depict."

"Hindustan," he writes, "is a country that has
few pleasures to recommend it."

Still he conquered it, pitting himself and his
northern hordes against the Rajputs finally at
Kanwaha near Agra. It was on this occasion that
Babar issued his total abstinence manifesto which
begins thus :—

"Gentlemen and Soldiers—whoso sits down to
the feast of life must end by drinking the cup of
death."

On this occasion he broke his golden drinking-cups
before the army, and poured out his stores of wine.

Nor did he afterwards break his vow, though but

a few years before he had written calmly, with the absolute frankness as to his faults which is so remarkable and so charming, "As I intended to abstain from wine at the age of forty, and as I now wanted somewhat less than a year of that age, I therefore drank wine most copiously."

Yet he could resist temptation, apparently, for we never hear of his being off duty, and we may be sure he would have mentioned the fact with perfect candour had he been so. Once when he was ill his diary is full of wisdom. It was easy to see, he writes, whence came his chastisement; he would abstain from idle thoughts and unseemly pleasures. He would even break his pen in penitence for the frivolous verse he had scribbled; yet but a few weeks later we find this entry: "The lights and watchfires in the valley seen from my tent were most extraordinarily beautiful; that is the reason, doubtless, why I drank too much wine at dinner."

When he died, Emperor of India at the age of forty-eight, they carried him back to his beloved hills, to the Garden of the New Year, where his mother lay, and wrote this on his tomb:

"Heaven is the eternal abode of the Emperor Babar."

7

It appears likely, for a more lovable, gifted, loyal, forgiving soul never visited this earth.

His son Humayun inherited most of his charm, but little of his capability. Chivalrous to a degree, brave as a lion, he lacked tenacity, and nearly let the empire slip through his fingers. The story of his eager return to help the Rani of Chitore when she made him her bracelet-brother and his dilatoriness in striking the needful blow for her safety is typical of him. So is that strange flight, almost alone, through the deserts of Sind, leading his young wife's palfrey and cheering her as best he could, till she could no more, and he had to leave her in a hill fortress, where, but a day or two afterwards, India's greatest king, in some ways her greatest man, the Emperor Akbar, was born. For eight years Humayun ruled with difficulty what his father had left him, for fourteen he waited an opportunity of regaining it, and within a year of once more getting the grip of conquest on the Panjab, he died, also at the fatal age of forty-eight. Highly educated, genial, extraordinarily witty, generous to a fault, Humayun nevertheless takes his place in history as the hander on of Babar's undoubted genius to Akbar.

Of the latter it is again difficult to speak too

KING BABAR'S TOMB .

highly. It is impossible to dismiss him as the Great Moghul, a figure-head indissolubly mixed up in most English minds with the Great Panjandrum and a pack of playing cards; for from whatever side we approach him, whether as man, soldier, philosopher, administrator, the conviction is forced home on us that we stand before one of those few really great men who have, as it were, revealed the future to their present age. In Babar there is genius; but it is genius trammelled, as it so often is, by instability. To use words which will be commonplaces in a few years, though somewhat theoretical to-day, his subliminal and his conscious selves were not on equal terms.

With Akbar they were, and he seems to have lived always master of himself. He was fourteen years old when he began to reign, and from that moment his grip was on all India.

His countenance, we are told by his son, "was full of godly dignity," and in person he must have resembled his grandfather Babar, as he was tall, handsome, strong, with exceedingly captivating manners. But in reading of his conquests, above all of his administrative reforms, one is struck most by the calm, cool courage with which he faced all difficulties, and the mastery not only of men, but of himself, which he displayed.

It is simply astounding to think how this boy of fourteen grasped at once the ephemeral nature of conquest without the cementing powers of mutual interests to bind conquerors and conquered together. For five years he seems to have dreamt this great dream, hitherto unknown to the world, of building up an empire, not on a foundation of swords, but on the goodwill of the people. To do this in a seething, swirling welter of races such as Hindostan—to make Mahommedan, Hindu, Buddhist, Jain equally content, to give all classes equal justice, to make them equally loyal to the State—this was no boy's work. But he set himself to it, and he succeeded. It is to be doubted indeed if Akbar's form of government is not to this day the one best fitted to the needs of India. There is small doubt, anyhow, that in the northern parts of India the great mass of the people refer to his age as a golden one ; for the memory of it is more consonant with their still primitive ideas than even our own more advanced, more civilised rule.

And yet Akbar was advanced, was civilised to an absolutely incredible extent. He is centuries before his time, and the number of laws passed by

him within a very few years of his accession at
fourteen years of age show a marvellous grasp on
what was needed to consolidate his vast empire.
Perfect religious freedom, the removal of obnoxious
taxation, a whole elaborate system of revenue
collection, the prohibition of suttee and female
infanticide, the legalisation of remarriage, and the
discountenancing of infant betrothal—all this, and
many another wise law, form a continuous procession of beneficial legislation which, emanating
not from a parliament of men, but from the brain
of one man only, and that a man whose surroundings were those of Eastern despotism and whose era
was that of Queen Elizabeth, is fairly astounding.

"The whole length and breadth of the land,"
writes Mahamed Amin of his reign, "was firmly
and righteously governed. All people of every
description and station came to his court, and
universal peace being established, men of every
sect dwelt secure under his protection."

He had, briefly, the power of independent
thought and the vitality which makes it possible
to turn thought to action. In other words, he
had genius.

The whole chronicle of his reign teems with
incidents of overwhelming interest as showing the

personality of this born ruler of men. Tall and
strong, he was counted the best polo-player in
India, while his abstemious life fitted him for the
extraordinary staying power which gave him an
almost uncanny reputation. On one occasion he
is known to have ridden eight hundred miles on
camel-back without rest, and to have been fit
thereafter to engage his enemy in battle.

But it is in the imagination of the man that his
greatest charm lies. He saw things, not as they
were, but as they should be. He lived in the face
of the Ideal, seeking above all things for the
Truth.

The record of his spiritual life culminates in his
creed :

O God! in every temple they seek Thee, in every language
they praise Thee; each religion says Thou art One.

Yet it is Thou whom I seek from Temple to Temple, since
heresy and orthodoxy stand not behind the Screen of the
Truth.

Heresy to the Heretic, Orthodoxy to the Orthodox; but
only the Dust of the Rose-petal remains for those who sell
Perfume.

This creed, the marvellous town of Fattehpore
Sikri, in which every building is a palace, every
palace a dream carved in red sandstone, and the
plain marble tomb with the single word '*Akbar*'

upon it under which the dead king lies in the florid mausoleum which Bishop Heber describes as "designed by Titans, finished by jewellers," will, as long as the world lasts, remain evidences of the most striking figure in Indian history. We have none to compare with it in England.

His son Jahangir lives only through the memory of his wife Nurjehan, the woman with whom he fell in love as a boy, and for whom he waited twenty years. His son, again, Shahjehan, lives through the presence of the Taj Mahal, which he built in memory of his wife, who died when her thirteenth child was born; a quaint instance, surely, of marital constancy in a Great Moghul which runs counter to many of the erroneous ideas which the West preconceives of the East.

Aurungzebe, the third of the second trio, reverted absolutely to orthodox Mahommedanism, and so broke up the empire which Babar won and Akbar consolidated.

CHAPTER VI

THE WESTERN RULERS

How many kings ruled after Aurungzebe signed the first treaty of peace with England, and Mr. Job Charnock, the *doyen* of Nabobs, landing on the left bank of the river Hooghly, laid the foundation of Calcutta ?

Who knows, and who cares. The first to begin the long line was one Bahadur Shah, the last to end it was also Bahadur Shah ; and between the two how many a vicissitude of power marked by the steadily increasing influence of the British merchants who came avowedly to exploit India !

For there can be no question that our empire in the East began with the "ultimate sixpence." That, and nothing else, was the *raison d'être* of our rule. It is not exactly edifying to read the history of those early years of steady encroachment for the sake of monetary gain ; indeed, out of the welter of intrigue, bribery, extortion, and overreaching, it is difficult to form any clear notion of what really did happen, and one is driven to judge of the action by its result.

And that was undoubtedly English aggression. From the year 1600, when a list was made of "the names of such persons as have written with their owne handes to venter in the splendid voiage to the Easte Indies (the which it maie please the Lorde to prosper)," until 1858, when Queen Victoria formally took over the Government, scarcely a year passed without some record of annexation. Bit by bit the land fell either to our pens or our swords, for we wielded both well and fearlessly.

Our first real essay with the latter was after the accession of James the Second, who, being a large shareholder of East India Company stock, was prepared to push the speculation by force of arms. Accordingly a thousand regulars and no less than two hundred guns were despatched with an elaborate plan of unprovoked attack on the coast about Chittagong. The attempt failed egregiously, and drew down on us the wrath of the Great Moghul, Aurungzebe, with whom eventually we made a nefarious and humiliating peace by offering up Sir John Child as an innocent scapegoat! After

8

this come fifty years during which the import of British goods doubled and trebled itself, so that the East India Company was in a position to lend a million to the English Government at 8 per cent in order to have their charter renewed. But by this time one Robert Clive had been born, and also one Warren Hastings, both men who were to make their mark in India. The former, by the overthrow of Suraj-ud-dowla at Plassey in 1757, sealed the fate of India. The less said of the diplomacy which led to the overthrow the better ; at the least, it was disingenuous to a degree, though for that Clive himself was not wholly responsible. Whether he was responsible for other and still more shady transactions it is hard to say ; if he were, he was at least no worse than his accusers. He was at any rate bold in his defence of himself; held to unwisdom, since by throwing out a challenge to his enemies he forced them to fight. But the whole story ending with Clive's death by his own hand in the depression of disease and disgrace—merited or unmerited, who can say—is a blot—a very dark blot—on the history of British India. It sickens one to read about it. And it was followed by another and almost similar stain due to the impeachment of Warren Hastings a

few years later. Were these two men, undoubtedly the greatest Englishmen of their time in India, both double-dyed scoundrels, or were they, as they claimed to be, only suffering from the resentment of scoundrels whose dishonesty they strove to check? Looking to the general state of affairs when the pagoda tree was still in full bearing and all that it required was a good shaking, it is to be feared that the theory which starts with but two just men is the most likely. These two, anyway, did something for what they gained, justly or unjustly. But whether exploited largely by two, or in lesser degree by two hundred, India was the sufferer, and as one reads the story of John Company's dealings with the natives, a feeling of shame creeps over one for many an unprovoked attack, many an absolutely dishonest piece of diplomacy. At the same time the record is one of steady, just administration, and, once a district or province was duly annexed, the extension to it of the laws and privileges which Englishmen had won for themselves by centuries of struggle.

Still, the fact remains that we met duplicity by greater duplicity. The early years of the nineteenth century witnessed the same system of absorption, and even so late as the fifties our absolutely unjust treatment of the Nawabs of Oude was largely responsible for the great Mutiny, —that, and the wave of Evangelical revival which swept across the continent of Europe in the late forties, and reaching India a few years later led to a sudden alteration in our attitude towards the people of India. The establishment of female schools, the sudden increase of missionary efforts, family prayers in which native servants had to join, the legislation of widow remarriage—a law which Akbar had enforced without any demur,— and many another similar evidence of a desire to save souls, roused a real terror lest Christianity should be forced upon India.

Of that great Mutiny, antedated by one month from the centenary of Plassey, a day which the whole of India had for years been secretly taught would see the end of British rule, pages might be written. It was at once a death throe and a birth throe, a record of the heroism of both races, an expiation on both sides for many evils in the past. It had to come. For once the white face and the dark had to meet in conflict over something better than the ultimate sixpence before they could find common ground of mutual respect. They were each fighting in 1857 for something that at bottom was dearer to them than gold or even land, and they emerged from the Valley of the Shadow with the clear eyes of those who have looked on death together.

Since those days India has travelled fast. Outwardly it is assimilating to itself our Western civilisation wholesale. Within? Who can say? Will the Eastern theory of life which asserts that Time, so far from being money, is naught, hold its own against our strenuous and deadly doing by which not one moment is left to a man wherein to *live.*

Again, who can say?

This much is certain—the most advanced thinkers of the West are day by day coming back to the philosophies of the East; so, perhaps the two great streams of thought, one surcharged with activities, the other with passivities, may meet, not in collision or absorption, but in an absolute welding together of all that is good and true in either.

CHAPTER VII

HINDUISM

BENARES still holds Hinduism past and present. In one of its wide old gardens, set thick, not so much with flowers as with flowering trees, there lived till lately a survival of the most ancient days of Hinduism; for Swami Baskeranund claimed to be a Vedic man—that is, a man whose spiritual life, based on the teaching of the Vedas, knew nothing of priests, or castes, or ceremonials. Certainly, he was a striking figure, and the very human vanity which led to his childish delight in his own marble statue, the very human perspicacity which made him invariably pick out those of the highest rank amongst his visitors for special favour, only emphasised the extraordinary expression of clear calm content upon his face. Almost naked, thin as an anatomy, hairless, toothless, there was such a dignity about him as doth hedge a king,

and the look in his eyes was exactly that of the
Child in the Madonna di San Sisto, a look of
wearied yet unwearied wisdom.

What then was the creed of this man ? Taking
him as an example of what Hinduism teaches in
the highest to its most apt pupils, it was the creed
of Aristotle, of Plato, Socrates, Buddha, the Christ
—the creed, that is, which comes again and again
to the world robed in a new white robe of salvation
for the sinner. He had already gone beyond the
veil of the flesh; he had found unity behind it in
the Holy-of-Holies. This sense of unity lies at
the bottom of all philosophies, all religions; they
do but voice man's eternal conviction of some
higher life in which his puny, futile one can be
merged. It is not a conception which appeals
much to the multitude, and so in India this funda-
mental belief is to be found overlaid with such a
supercargo of superstition and crazy creeds that it
is sometimes difficult to see that it exists.

But it does. The veriest coolie, if hard pressed,
will tell you that even your Honour's anger is all
" *Maya* " or illusion, and that the reality lies elsewhere; where, being a matter which scarcely con-
cerns him, poor creature of a day. For all that, his
mortal life is a perfect prey to such illusions, and

the number of sanctions and limitations which he has to consider before he can get through a single day of it decently is perfectly appalling. These took possession of him long ere he was born, when his father and mother, in honour of his expected arrival, performed various ceremonies, the Uncooked-Food ceremony, the Cooked-Food ceremony, and finally the Feast-of-the-Five-Gifts, when milk, clarified butter, curds, honey, and cow dung are worshipped as the food of the gods.

There is a belief prevalent amongst Europeans that every Hindu has to be born in a cow-house. If this were so, it would still be no more hardship than the birth of the Christ in a stable; but it is not the case. The mother, being ceremonially unclean, cannot remain in the house, and therefore finds refuge in some building or lumber room, where she stays until the days of her purification are over. The seventh night after birth, Brahma, in his Wisdom-form, is supposed to come and write its fate upon the child's forehead. The following ceremonials vary with every caste, every race; but the name-giving, in which the father writes the name with a golden ring in unhusked rice, is curiously persistent; its persistency pointing to some now-forgotten symbolism. The ceremony of giving the child its first grain of rice when it is six months old is also a great festival ; and so is the shaving of its head into the orthodox scalp lock, and the beginning of its education. For the latter, on some auspicious day agreed upon by the family priest, friends and relatives are called together, and with varying customs and rites the child, if it be a boy, is handed over to a teacher, who, invoking the aid of the gods, teaches his pupil the form of the first vowel by drawing it once more in un-husked rice.

Amongst Brahmans, however, the great festival of a boy's life is the day on which he is invested with the *zonar*, or sacred thread of second birth. Worn over the left shoulder, it is twisted of cotton wool and silk, and is the dearest possession of the priestly race. With it goes the right of repeating the sacred text, which is always whispered so that no other can hear it :

"Oṁ! O! Earth, O! Air, O! Heaven Oṁ! Let us meditate on the supreme splendour of the Divine Sun, and may His Light lighten us."

This ceremony over, the child starts fair on its life as an orthodox Hindu, and for the most part leads the life of an apprentice to learning until the age of sixteen is reached. For Hinduism divides

9

the life of man into four divisions or ages—Disciple-
ship, Husbandhood, Parenthood, Saintship.   In the
first age you learn, in the second love and the world
claim you, in the third your children, in the fourth
the world beyond.   So you pass out of one life into
the next.

To a Hindu man or woman marriage is a
solemn religious duty.   It is an absolutely inviolable sacrament, and divorce is unknown; the
underlying theory being that before God the male
and the female form together the perfect human
being.   Therefore neither can really worship apart
from the other.   Before such a belief as this, it is
idle to talk of the woman's position being degraded.
It is not so in theory, whatever it may be in
practice.   Indeed, to any one who really thinks
upon the vexed question of the relationship between
the sexes, the Hindu standpoint is the only one
that affords a stable foothold.   For, once we allow
personal passion its right on marriage, the difficulty
of finding any point on which to cry " Halt "
becomes apparent.

Once married, a Hindu almost invariably becomes a perfect prey to his women folk, at any
rate for some years.   So many things are lucky,
so many unlucky, that life tends to be one long

propitiation or praise, festival or fast. It is astonishing to what lengths the woman's influence may go, and many an accurately dressed Europeanised native may carry about with him, carefully concealed, some ludicrous or even horrible talisman against evil spirits in which, were you to ask him, he would deny belief. He might also deny the efficacy of pilgrimages, but he goes on them, and the thirty and odd big festivals which raise his whole household to a pitch of pleasurable excitement during the year, find him quite ready to take his part in them. It is a quaint background to his self-contained semi-European life as clerk or merchant, lawyer or doctor. Yet it exists, and the man who has pled his case in court with a legal etiquette acquired in England, or spent his day over the commerce of many continents, may end it by wreathing the Goddess of Smallpox with strung flowers, or even by bathing in some dreadful admixture of the Five Gifts.

And yet under all the turmoil of almost senseless worship, behind all the thirty thousand and odd deities which are so worshipped in India, there is not one Hindu from Cape Cormorin to the Himalayas who would not scout the idea of there being more Gods than One, and that One Unknow-

able, Mysterious, Absolute Holiness. The rest
are but Ideas, founded by man in the vain effort
to bring the Incomprehensible into compre-
hension.

Beyond this unalterable belief, and the belief in
Maya or Illusion, there is no dogma in Hinduism.
And *Maya* is the illusion of personality, of individualism. The whole universe is God, all things
are forms of Him, yet men claim individual life,
think of themselves as apart from Him. This is
Maya. To escape from it is to realise Unity, to
find oneself in all things, and all things in God.
This is Nirvana.

So we come back to the philosophers of all ages,
to the secret of all religions, to the merging of a
puny individual life in the Greater one of Greater
Dimensions. That this view of ourselves, our life,
should necessarily lead to quietism, is the belief of
the Western nations, to whom deadly doing and
the gospel of personal comfort are a religion in
themselves; but it is an erroneous belief, for once
beyond the galling limitations of merely individual
life the whole activities of the world are yours, and
the blossoming of a flower, the glad song of the
bird, the hammering on an ironclad's side, and the
great cry for freedom which goes up from man-

kind are all equal harmonies in the symphony of existence.

It is a boundless horizon, but it is one which the Hindu has ever before his eyes, despite the multiplicity of his gods, and the endless tale of ceremony which compass him about on every side.

A Brahman, if he desires to perform his religious rites properly, should spend at least five hours a day over them, so complex have become the rules for ablution, expiation, and purification; and yet his aim is, as a great missionary writes almost contemptuously, "to obtain knowledge which will ensure his reunion with God."

The belief in life after death is general amongst Hindus. Heaven for a longer or shorter period awaits the soul which has striven towards the light, hell the soul which has chosen darkness. Then once more comes another chance, another reincarnation. So the wheel with its two pivots of birth and death turns, until the soul, escaping from the illusion, the limitations of personality, finds rest in the perfection of the Supreme. The process may last for millions of years, but, in the end, as all things have emanated from God, to Him they will return.

There is a legend that the gods having by pious acts obtained immortality, Yama, the Ender, the God of Death, came to them and said :

> " As ye have made yourselves
> Imperishable, so will men endeavour
> To free themselves from me ; what portion then
> Shall I possess in man ? "   The gods replied,
> " Henceforth no being shall become immortal·
> In his own body ; this his mortal frame
> Shalt thou still seize ; this shall remain thine own.
> He who through knowledge or religious works
> Henceforth attains to immortality,
> Shall first present his body, Death, to thee." [1]

It is this absolute certainty of a future life which generates the disregard of death that is so marked a feature in Indian life.   It is no stranger whom the Hindu awaits as he lies on the bare earth from which he came, while those who have been his companions in this particular incarnation wait also, commending his soul to the care of Râm.   Death is a familiar friend in whose embrace he has already lain many, many times.

This disregard of death is never more strikingly shown than during a cholera epidemic.   Then, when a whole cantonment will be in a state of panic, the hospitals full of spurious cases due largely

---

[1] Wilkins, *Indian Wisdom.*

to pure fright, when the authorities are doing all they can by various amusements to keep up the spirits of the Europeans, the native city hard by, where the disease rages unchecked by cantonment regulations, will go on its way calmly, burying and burning its dead by the hundred without one sign of fear.

I remember in one village of three hundred souls all told, where a passing pilgrim from Hardwar sickened with cholera, and as a result there were eighty-five deaths within thirty-six hours, the only complaint made was that the pilgrim himself recovered! That was considered rather unfair.

This stoicism in regard to suffering and death is apt to engender a certain hardness in those who are witness to it. During the retreat from Afghanistan, for instance, when cholera broke out amongst our troops, it was not till a British regiment was attacked that prayers were offered up for the staying of the plague in our churches, though for six weeks previously the native regiments had been suffering terribly. And yet, if the ordinary missionary view be accepted, they were in more parlous straits than their Christian brethren.

But, in truth, the Hindu standpoint is a very hard one to attack. Practically all proselytising must be directed against the intolerable mass of superstition and ceremonial which has grown up round its central idea; for the only appeal against that must be an appeal to selfishness, to the desire to carry ourselves and all our petty narrow interests into a future world.

CHAPTER VIII

MAHOMMEDANISM

MAHOMMEDANS in India number about one-fifth of
the total population.   Roughly speaking, therefore,
the count is one to every three Hindus.   They are,
however, by no means evenly distributed, nearly
one-half of them being found in Bengal and con-
siderably more than one-half of the remainder in
the Punjab; that is, at either end, as it were, of
the great waves of Central Asian conquests which
swept down the Gangetic plain again and again.

With the exception of enforced converts from
the Jât and Rajput races, all the Indian Mahommedans are, like ourselves, alien to the soil.   They
are also of extremely varied extraction.   Scythians,
Tartars, Moghuls, Belooch, Persians, Afghans, and
half a score of other races still remain curiously
intact, stranded by the receding tide, and still
preserving their original type.

For as the Hindus were quick to adopt the
Moslem custom of secluding women, so by that
swift interchange of bad habits which it is to be
feared is generally the result of man's close companionship, the Mahommedans immediately adopted
caste restrictions; with the result that intermarriage
between different tribes became rare.

So to this day, the hawk-nosed, eagle-eyed
descendants of true Arab descent can almost be
recognised at first sight; and the broad-faced,
massive-featured Belooch can scarcely be mistaken
for his taller, slenderer neighbour the Jât.

But amongst the whole of them, except perhaps
the higher classes of Delhi Moghuls or Oude
Syuds, it is impossible to find a social comity of
purely Mahommedan type. Indeed, to such an
extent are they riddled by and permeated with
Hinduism that even virgin widowhood, than which
nothing could be found more repugnant to the
whole teaching of Islam, obtains amongst some
tribes, and all, without exception, while refusing to
eat food from the hands of the One-God-worship-
ping Christian, take it freely from the idolatrous
Hindu; the teaching of Mahommed, of course,
being the other way about!

They are undoubtedly the poorest people in

India—poorest and most debased; in the large towns a prey to well-worn evil and much-inherited disease. In the country, on the other hand, there is often little to choose between Hindu and Mahommedan neighbours, except that the latter are less enterprising, less educated, more proud. There is, in fact, amongst them a certain sadness of decay, a clinging to past traditions, a feeling that they have come down in the world. Now and again you come upon a colony of them, living in some old many-storied town, surrounded by the mere mounds of ruined broken brick which tell of some larger city in the olden time, and feel a pang of pity for the departed glory of both place and people. Everything, even the gold-tissue tunic in which the head of the clan turns out to receive you, is frayed and worn; the very children, large-eyed, solemn, play the old games decorously in the gutter. Nowhere is this lack of any keen interest in life to be seen so clearly as in Delhi. There, in some quarters, the town is a town almost of the dead. The tall houses seek the sky, shutting out the sunlight; a shrouded woman creeps through the shadows; a group of half-drowsy men sit, objectless, in the wide doorways, blocked, almost barricaded, by a transverse brick screen. There is a

stagnant pool of indescribable filth at your feet,
fed by slimy trickles down the purple pock-marked
walls, whence the smaller bricks have dropped,
leaving hollows in the mortar. The droning sound
of some one chanting the Koran filters out through
narrow latticed windows. Here and there, farther
down the narrow lane, a stain of vivid blue or red
on the uneven brick pavement tells that some one
upstairs has been saving twopence by dying cloth
at home.

But there are few pennies to spare among the
inhabitants of these high tenement-houses. How
some of them gain their living at all is a mystery.
Sometimes you come upon an old man sitting in
the dusty sun-ray which slants through the long
slip of a room—a room empty, save at the corners,
where lie huddled bundles and baskets containing
Heaven knows what! He is weaving tinsel threads
at a diminutive loom—weaving it in some old, half-
forgotten way; and on the proceeds of this a
whole family of children and grandchildren manage
to live. Or, hard at work, some patriarchal household may be seen busy stitching away at caps or
embroidering shoes. Such work is the refuge of
the decayed Mahommedan courtier. They are very
pious, often very depraved, and their very festivals

are solemn. The fate of their women when they are left alone in the world is very terrible. No prisoner condemned to a life sentence leads a harder, more joyless existence than many a king's daughter has spent in some back slum in Delhi, grinding away from morning till evening at the corn mill, that last exchange of stones for bread which there is in India. Some years ago there were over seven hundred pensioners of the Crown, most of them women, in Delhi. Half of them never saw a penny of the money monthly doled out to some distant relative, and the other half were contented with some poor percentage of what was granted to them for compensation, because—as one of them said cheerfully to me, "my husband was hanged by mistake in the Evil Day." Poor souls, what redress had they against the responsible man? And in truth the male pensioner is apt to be a terror, whether he takes the form of an old Turk with red dyed beard and an infinite distrust of women-kind, or a dicing, gambling, quail-fighting young one, who spends his nights in the bazaar and the days in lolling capless, turbanless on a bedstead set in the doorway.

It is in Lucknow, however, that you touch bottom, as it were, in the lees of a dead court. In that town of stucco and sham, vice itself takes on a hideous unreality, there is a slackness in wickedness itself, but it is the slackness of a sleeping snake which has still poison in its fang, is still ready to strike if it finds opportunity.

And, as one reads the history of Lucknow, wonder passes; for surely never did degradation do its work more fully than in those last days of royalty. The very children bear the traces of it still, and yet in many a ruined old house in Lucknow lonely women are living still whose patient continuance in well-doing is a marvel indeed.

For of that there is no doubt. The Mahommedan woman of good family is often a compendium of all the most Christian virtues. Her patience is phenomenal. She is content to take the lowest place in this life and the next.

In the country, however, matters are brighter, both for the man and the woman. Though a Mahommedan is seldom, if ever, so good a cultivator of the soil as a Hindu, he can still hold his own with them, while as a breeder of horses or cattle he is their superior.

But even at his best the Mahommedan never looks so happy and contented as the Hindu. His religion does not really offer him so much consolation. A heaven full of houris, an eternal procession of sensual pleasures (which experience in this world proves to be provocative of headache), is not a very exhilarating outlook for any staid man of middle age. Then in Mahommedan houses, as elsewhere in India, the grey mare is so often the better horse, and there is such kindly affection between husband and wife, that the theory of a merely problematical Paradise by means of a husband's coat-tail for the woman, is not satisfactory.

But, thank Heaven! it is for the most part but a theory.

There are many fewer festivals for the Mahommedan than for the Hindu, and they are mostly of rather a funereal character.

Mohurrum, for instance, is instinct with weeping, wailing, and fiercest religious feeling. Shab-i-barat, with its touching feast for all those who have died in the past, is no time for jollity. Eed-ul-Fitr, the day which breaks the fast of Ramzan, comes nearest to our idea of a festival, but on all the five great days of the year religious services and the preparation of food for the poor occupy a large portion of the time.

There is one great disadvantage attached to the Mahommedan religion in India: it does not enjoin daily ablution as a religious service. Consequently, especially amongst the poorer classes, dirt is a very common failing, whereas personal cleanliness is the rule amongst Hindus.

Undoubtedly, taken *en masse*, the Mahommedan is not at his best in India. His star is not in the ascendant, and his position wars with his religion. That enjoins conversion by the sword if need be, and an almost fierce intolerance of the idolater. His whole *entourage* therefore is galling, and the friction shows itself in a lower moral standard in the many. The few, as always, rise above circumstances, and there are no better men and women in India than some Mahommedans.

CHAPTER IX

BUDDHISM, JAINISM, PARSEEISM, ANIMISM

THERE are, roughly speaking, three million Buddhists in India, one and half million Jains, and over seven million non-Aryan aboriginal tribes of practically no religion at all.

The Buddhists are to be found almost entirely fringing the hilly outskirts of the empire. Their hold has gone from the plains, where such magnificent memorials as the tope at Sanchi remain to show that they had once a grip on the whole land. But Brahmanism with its elaborate system of caste prevailed—as it was bound to prevail, owing to its appeal to the family, the racial feeling in humanity. Still from one end to another of India the teaching of Sakyamuni are the foundations of all spiritual life. Between the conclusions of Hinduism and Buddhism at their highest there is little to choose: in both the claims of personality are the root of all evil; in both salvation lies in the realisation of unity.

The same thing may be said of the Jains—indeed, of all Eastern religions. All press the claims of collectivism over those of individualism. But the Jaina religion smacks of extreme antiquity. We are told that it was founded by Rishaba Deva, and a date is added subsequent to the time of Buddha; but internal evidence points to one of the oldest faiths in the world. The use of the Swastika or Fylfot alone would make one hesitate to place Jainism a century or so before Christ; for the Swastika is the oldest known symbol in the world and the most widespread. Its quaint cross, like an Isle of Man crest with four feet, is to be found from Scandinavia to Polynesia, from Africa to America. Mysterious utterly—for the ends at right angles to the uprights could have been derived from no mere savage crossing of sticks—the unriddling of its first meaning will be the unriddling of many problems. Of course, the solar mythists have claimed it, as they claim all else; but the fact that it is universally an emblem of good luck, that it is used as an equivalent for womanhood, and that it is inextricably mixed up with the serpent, points to another origin.

But it is old, old as Time itself, and with the Jains it is still the sign *par excellence.*

Another peculiarity of the Jains is their extreme consideration for life. Some of their ascetics go through life with their nostrils and mouth swathed in muslin, lest by chance they should inhale and so destroy some frail inhabitant of the air. Luckily the microscope was unknown to them, else still stricter precautions, resulting in death to the breather, might have to be taken. The Jains divide themselves into two camps—the "Sky-clad ones" and the "White-robed ones." Of the two, those who, clad in the sky, go naked, or at least eat their food naked, are the stricter, possibly the most ancient. One curious tenet of theirs, that no woman by any means or at any time can ever attain to Nirvana, goes far to prove their antiquity, and, connected as this belief is with the use of the Swastika, raises many speculations.

The Jains are a very opulent people. Their horror of shedding the blood of even an insect has restricted them largely to sedentary occupations. It has, indeed, handicapped them in the activities of life, and legend says that the last Jaina king lost his kingdom through a refusal to march his army one night in the rains, because of the enormous sacrifice of insect life which must have ensued. Be that as it may, their energies diverted largely into commerce and banking, have placed them as the richest community in India, with the exception, perhaps, of the Parsees.

There is a large colony of Jain bankers and merchants in Delhi, at Jeypore, Ahmedabad, and indeed in almost every town in Rajputana. In Delhi one may often in the Jain quarter, quiet, secluded, almost asleep in the sunlight, hear the quaint cry of the wicked, impish little Mahommedan boys and girls who, having caught a sparrow, go with it from house to house threatening to kill and enforcing ransom. Indeed, seeing the ease with which these little bird-slayers, as they are called, extort halfpence with their cry, "Ai! followers of Rishaba! give or I kill," the wonder rises why this system of toll is not practised in larger matters. For all we know it may be.

The Jain architecture is some of the finest in India. Their cave temples are numerous, and in almost every large town some building, exquisite in the fineness of its carving, stands sponsor to the wealth and religion of the Jains. Their holy place, which at the same time shows the most perfect specimen of their art, is Mount Abu. Here is to

be found a group of temples served by the strictest sect of sky-clad *sad'hus*, who never marry, who practise the utmost asceticism, and in their care for animal life sweep the ground before them with a broom ere they set foot on it.

The Parsees are another rich race. In Bombay they are outwardly even more European than the Europeans; but within, the old faith of the fire-worshippers remains, less touched by Western thought than Hinduism is in Calcutta. The concrete belief in Hormuzd, the Central Creator typified in the sun, and in the sun's vicegerent, fire, is one that fits in better with Western forms of thought than do the more mystical abstractions of Hindu philosophy.

Beyond these religions—in which Sikhism might have found a place, but for its rapid reassimilation into the Brahmanical form of Hinduism, even to the extent of a re-recognition of the caste system—we have the seven and a half millions or so of non-Aryan tribes who are Animists, Shamanists—in other words, devil-worshippers. If we add to this those partially Hinduised or Mahommedanised races whom we used to call Pariahs—the leather-workers, sweepers, basket-makers, fowl-keepers of India—we get the large total of nearly eighteen millions who are practically of no known religion at all. It is from amongst them—as might have been expected —that Christianity has gained most of its converts.

Their belief, as a rule, goes no further than some dim idea of a distant god who has committed the charge of this world to demons and ghosts who have to be pacified, outwitted if possible. In the old days human sacrifices were a common form of propitiation. Once a year in almost every village or group of villages a young man was offered up for the good of the many. Nowadays the ceremony goes on as ever, and, according to what one is told, as effectively, but with great secrecy and many precautions against police interference. A bit of the chosen victim's hair has to be secured privately, a morsel of his clothing. These, with due ritual, are placed in the wide brazen platter surrounded by the sacrificial fire, while the shivery, teeth-chattering villagers circle in the shadow watching, waiting. And, sure enough, ere long the few hairs, the shreds of cloth, visualise themselves into the very semblance of the owner, and from out of the shadows pounces the demon, teeth whetted for the dreadful feast.

With more shivers, more chattering of teeth, the villagers watch it in silence, and then go home.

The devil's hunger is assuaged—the victim will die within the year, and the white faces cannot object to the judgment of God.

The existence of such simple souls—and in such large numbers—within the great continent of India makes the problem of its political future almost overwhelmingly difficult. Young Bengal clamours for a vote; perhaps justly. But are we to give it to the Santhal, the Bhil, the Kasya? Or if we give it not, what is to be the test of fitness? Literacy? Then half the men whose vote is most worth having, the steady cultivators of the soil, the landed proprietors, the men of weight and influence— would be excluded in favour of a "middell-faili"— the man who has gone up for the middle school examination and failed for it.

Not yet! we have not come to that yet—thank Heaven!—in India.

CHAPTER X

WHAT is the scent of a bazaar?

Who can say? It is quite indescribable, that fatty not unpleasant smell which is compounded, one knows, of so many unpleasant things; for instance, drains, humanity, assafœtida. Taking it as a whole, however, I fancy the smell of turmeric brings back more than anything else the wonderful kaleidoscope of colours in an Indian bazaar. Take the Almond Bazaar, for instance, at Lahore. Looking down its long, narrow length, its infinite variety of tint and form is the first thing which strikes a stranger. And yet there is really very little variety in the wares for sale, or indeed in the shops where they are sold. There is, of course, always the shifting, changing crowd, giving the glare of an orange turban here, the gleam of a red petticoat there; but for the rest, a description of a

dozen or so of shops would exhaust the whole of them.

First and foremost the grain-sellers. Under a cavernous toothed arch the pyramid-piled baskets of various peas, wheat, barley, grain, flour, sugar, chillies, curry stuffs, rise in a slanting heap backed by the dealer himself armed with a big pair of scales. That is a daily customer coming for his quantity of coarse flour. It is weighed out in a second, tilted into the corner of the customer's shawl, a tiny piece of rock salt added free of charge, and a penny changes hands. Possibly, if the buyer be fairly well to do, a smear of clarified butter, or a spoonful of sour milk curd in a green-leaf cup, will be carried away also. So, one man's hunger will be satisfied for that day. The next customer may have larger wants, and ere he leaves even the tail-end of his turban may be occupied by little knotted bags of sugar, rice, split peas, and he may have in addition a paper corne or two, tied about with cotton thread, of spices and perhaps tea. For the bunniah sells almost everything that can be cooked into food—dried fruits, potatoes, and all kinds of quaint nuts and flour pastes, like our Western vermicelli; *soojee*, too, that is the innermost germ of wheat, which is made by moistening

12

the whole grain and grinding it in a stone picked out into minute holes, is another of his wares.

He will lend money also to any one who asks him for it on no security, but a perfectly appalling rate of interest per day; and in the long flat box, blackened with age, on which he sits, he has most likely got quite a pile of silver ornaments waiting to be taken out of pawn.

⤬ The next shop may be a goldsmith's. It is only a tiny mud-plastered square with a little mud-brázier in the middle, at which the occupant blows with his blow-pipe, but he will tell you the percentage of alloy in your gold watch-chain in a moment with his touchstone, and guess the weight of the diamond in your ring to a *ratti*. He has a marvellously delicate set of scales in a little sandal-wood box, and the most confusing set of weights in the world —tiny scraps of glass, a bean perhaps, an irregular chunk of some metal, a bit of stick, a red and black seed, an odd morsel of turquoise, and a thin leaf of mother-o'-pearl. Anything and everything comes handy to the goldsmith's scales, and he remembers, or says he remembers, the weight of each, and totals them up in his head, saying as he weighs an earring or bracelet, "That will be one tola, two mashas, four ruttis, and a poppy

seed; with the making thereof, four rupees, eight annas, nine pie."

No wonder the broad-faced country woman who has brought her store of silver to be fashioned wrinkles her forehead in perplexity and acquiesces with a sigh.

A goldsmith, as the saying goes, would cheat his own mother on the scales, and many are the stories of his overreaching himself in this way which are current amongst the people—ay! and which are cast at him across the mud-plastered floor of his shop should dispute run high. But in one way there is security from the wiles of the goldsmith: he cannot work in alloys, and even when using coined metal has to treat it again and again with quicksilver so as to make it soft and ductile.

Next door is a pansari's or druggist's shop. Here, surely, is the most curious olla-podrida of wares the world ever saw under one archway! And there are thousands more inside the dark cavern beyond the arch, stowed away in little screws of paper, which in their turn are hidden out of sight and dust in earthen pots, or reed baskets, or pigeon-holes, or any and every kind of receptacle. He also has a substratum of shallow baskets heaped with turmeric, ochres of different sorts, red Holi powder, black salt and peppers. He has opium too, and charras and bhang, selling these on a Government licence. Dried violets are also part of his stock-in-trade, and in the early morning customers will come to him for "Epsom Sar'l," "Sidlis," or even "Eno's Fruit Salt." Later on in the day some old Mahommedan will take the drug-seller into his confidence, and together they will work out some occult and partially nefarious prescription—rose leaves, the shining spiculæ from the inside of a bamboo stem, pigeon's dung, and Heaven knows what!—all of which *pansari-ji* will produce; for it is almost as much a shibboleth with him to have everything in stock, as it is with William Whiteley's, Limited. I myself have asked one for cuttle-fish bone, and lo! there it was, just two or three small broken pieces in a paper screw. If the *pansari-ji* be—which is but seldom—a Mahommedan, he may look on himself as a hakim or doctor also, in which case he will not only dispense medicines, including the celebrated Thirty-Six powder, which is supposed to cure thirty-six diseases, but will charge a few annas for mystic talismans written with many cantrips on betel leaves or scraps of paper, the same having to be rolled into pills or swallowed whole without water.

On the whole, life would be impossible in India without the pansari. Has a horse a sore back, to him do you go for alum and indigo. Have you rheumatism, he will produce a tiny bottle of lemon grass oil. Do you feel the spring-time in your blood, he will mix you a kala-dana draught which will be a positive illness for days and reduce you many pounds in weight! For the pansari does things thoroughly while he is about it, and it is always safer to halve his doses of native medicine. He will, or at any rate he used to, sell you a pound of crude arsenic without a wink, and the aconite root from his shop is of uncertain strength. For how many deaths he is responsible during the year, who can say; but he brings much comfort into life, for, when the early morning hours with their bustle of "yet another day" are over, there is quite a little crowd round his shop, and the purchasers go away cheerfully with their little screws of paper which contain the Dream Compeller.

Next to him, perchance, stands the shop of a cloth merchant. This is palatial in comparison, monopolising two or even three arches, and the piles of Manchester goods rise in columns from the floor, receding backwards in aisles that end in darkness. The floor is spread with white calico

over a worn drugget, and two or three cane stools
await the more distinguished customers; but the
country women in for a day's shopping squat on a
string bed set over the gutter and haggle for hours
over the price of a new pair of baggy trousers for
the bride of the family. The cloth merchant
himself has a variety of manners—one especially
kept, with a schedule of prices, for the sahib logue,
to whom he will talk learnedly of "matchin'"
and "tintin'"; the "latest fashshun," alas! having
already filtered down to the string bed over the
gutter where Chand Kaur and Parbutti are arguing
the relative styles of yellow and red, and yellow
and green *sussi*. On the whole, Manchester
goods are cheaper in the cloth merchant's shop
than they are in Manchester itself, while the choice
is far greater. It is, indeed, sad to see the piles on
piles of absolute rubbish glazed with dressing into
the semblance of solidity, skimped by a half-inch
here, a half-yard-in-the-piece there, dyed with
ephemeral aniline dyes, or printed in flaring flowers,
which are replacing the more sober strength of
Indian manufactures. It is only the old women
now who finger the flimsy fabrics and murmur of
English "starch." But even the young ones still
favour the white piece goods of Germany, because

A BAZAAR AT PESHAWUR

.   •

the *measure is always right*. For our rivals in
commerce are quicker-witted than we are, and
recognise the value of considering the fancy of
their market; one of these fancies being that the
piece shall hold its good forty yards.

Then there are columns of cheap woollen cloths,
mostly shoddy and of the most brilliant hues; and
in those thinner piles showing much paper there
are even horrible *ponjee* silks scarcely to be differentiated from the paper which holds them. Some,
slightly better, have a narrow striped border imitat-
ing the native-made silks, which they are gradually
ousting; and amongst them are pieces of so-called
gold tissues—horrible tinselly things, which will
make a fine show in a wedding trousseau, and
thereinafter turn black and go rotten.

So a cloth merchant's shop is not altogether
exhilarating, except to a budding politician, who
might learn more from it than he might care to
learn. Still, even here, if you hint a desire to |see
something less civilised, Lalla-ji will say to an
underling, "Fetch out the bundle we had from
Samarkhand," or Benares, or Ispahan, and there,
carefully done up in cotton casing against the moth,
and the still greater pest, the woolly insect, will be
things worth buying,—a piece of gauzy-gold-

embroidered silk muslin, an invertebrate shine of old gold satin facing both ways, a few yards of silver shimmer on a violet ground.

"There is no one to buy," remarks Lalla-ji; "even the noble people sing cheap nowadays."

But the taste of India is not quite ruined yet; for a hush falls on the string bed set in the gutter, while Chand Kaur and Parbutti let the Manchester fabrics fall from their listless fingers, as they eye the "bundle from Samarkhand" wistfully.

Let us purchase, if it be but one square inch of honest beauty, and go on our way amid the smiles of the onlookers. For never was such a sympathetic audience as the one in an Indian bazaar. It is ready always to chime in with the claims of the customer and to give remonstrant advice to the seller—to shake its head philosophically over a bad, and rejoice over a good bargain.

I remember once having a dispute in what is called a "box wallah's" shop—that is, a shop which sells haberdashery, soap, brushes, combs, writing-paper, babies' bottles, and Cockle's pills—over a hank of native floss silk, the only one in the shop of a peculiar apricot tint. The price asked was eight annas, and despite the support of a slowly gathering crowd I was unable to reduce it to the

normal six. I therefore asked the shopkeeper to give me six annas' worth, hoping he would do as he did—that is, divide the hank in two, and proceed to roll my share up in paper. A blank disappointment settled on the faces of my audience. It was palpable injustice, but *quoi faire?*

What a change there was, however, when, as if I had altered my mind, I took up the remaining half, and saying, "After all, I think I only want two annas' worth," transferred it to my bag. A roar of unextinguishable laughter, in which the "bocus wallah" joined, rose up into the yellow sunlight.

I think it is dealing so much with civilised articles, such as trouser buttons, which debauches the "bocus wallah," but strangers and pilgrims had better beware of him unless they know the proper price of what he sells. Still he has his good points. He is the only man on God's earth who never runs short of "Rowland's Macassar Oil," although the putting of oil on the hair went out somewhere in the fifties. He always has a supply at "store prices."

A few steps farther and we are back in ancient India. This is a *bhunja's* shop, and there is nothing in it at all—nothing but a wide, shallow, round, cup-shaped iron pan set in the mud platform which forms, as it were, a counter. But beneath this counter is an oven-like fireplace, and the dark, wide-featured woman behind it is feeding the furnace with dry leaves and husks. What a delicious smell there is, and how the corn, which another woman stirs in the pan with a bundle of twigs, pops and fluffs out to whiteness. As they pass, people throw a pice on the mud counter and hold out some portion of their raiment, and to it comes a handful of parched maize, or wheat, or gram, which they munch as they go along. Half India lives on parched grain. It is a vice, like snuff-taking or cigarette-smoking, and the very babies nibble away at it. With a drink of water, it satisfies the Aryan brother for many hours; that is one reason why, as a soldier, he marches better in a hard country than Tommy Atkins, for a pound of parched grain can be tied up in the end of his turban, be tucked into its folds—giving him an inch or two of height—and there he is, without need of a baggage train for twenty-four hours.

The next shop may be a greengrocer's, though, for the most part, they prefer a stall in some open market where the great piles of melons lie like pumpkins. There is no more uncertain fruit in

the world than an Indian melon. You may cut
in to a hundred, and each one of them will taste
faintly of rhubarb and magnesia.   The hundred
and first, outwardly the same, will be food for the
gods.   But the populace is not very particular.
A melon is a melon, and it is good to be in the
bazaar when they are in full season, when the laden
donkeys unburden sacks of them on the brick pavement, and the very babies in arms are chewing
away at a chunk.   There are very few Indian
fruits worth eating ; even the mangosteen is over-
rated, and one can quite understand the Emperor
Babar's regret for the peaches and grapes of his
little far-away kingdom of Ferghana.   Of course,
there are some people who can eat jack fruit ; but
others will walk half a mile to keep to windward
of it.   Guavas are also a trial to some folk ; and,
personally, I can see no reason why there should be
railway carriages reserved "for Europeans only,"
except that native gentlemen and ladies like to
eat guavas, jack fruits, and chew *pán*, in season
and out of season.

A great buzzing of flies proclaims the next shop
to be a confectioner's. It is a pretty large shop,
with a tiered mud-counter on one side and possibly
a sugar-boiling furnace on the other, where the

metai-wallah is busy pulling out candy or making *butté-sas* on a hot plate. The latter when fresh are really quite nice, being, as it were, merely a bubble of milk and sugar. *Jellabis* are also excellent, if you can persuade the maker to fry the batter in good instead of bad butter. *Burfâni* is nothing but cream toffee plastered with silver leaf; and *réwerah*, small candy or rock cakes thickly covered with husked linseed and slightly flavoured with spices, are well worth attention. Then there are endless varieties of *luddu*, made of sugar and curded milk. They, being the cheapest of sweets, are the standby of the poor. Give a street child a farthing, he will spend it, for sure, on two big round balls of sugar, *ghi*, and pounded pulse, or, if he is an epicure, on two smaller sweet fritters. If he is hungry, however, he will go in for a whole two ounces of *hulwa*, a dry combination of flour, sugar, and *ghi*, in which the flour predominates. The whole population has a sweet tooth of perfectly preposterous size, and a grown man going on a journey is sure as a preliminary to pay a visit to the confectioner's. Since trade is brisk, the latter nearly always looks contented as he sits perfunctorily whisking away the flies from his wares. It is a vain task. They fill

VEGETABLE MARKET, DELHI

the air, and settle on your face with sticky, sugary feet as you pause to look.

The next arch is probably a sherbet-seller's, since sweets are thirsty food. In the old days the whole *mise en scène* consisted of five or six bottles or jars, a drinking-vessel of copper, a pile of fragile pottery bowls, and a pitcher of clear water; but nowadays, when folk are not so particular as to what they drink out of, four or five green-glass tumblers answer all purposes when wiped round the edge with a bit of paper, and there is a row of lemonade, ginger ale, and soda water behind them. It is to be doubted also if the bottles contain only, as they used to contain, lemon and tamarind syrup, violet essence, and such like. Doubtless these are asked for still on hot days, and some old customers still come for a glass of sugared water with just a smear of sandal-wood oil round the edge of the cup; but in many cases the sherbet-seller's is frankly a drink-shop, and young India may be seen seated on cane stools outside, smoking cigarettes and drinking whisky and soda.

An old Mahommedan, lean, wizened, coming for his daily draught of *banafsha* sherbet, will edge round their modern skirts gingerly, and mayhap say "Tobah!" under his breath. Yet no amount of penitence, no abjuration of the few—and for the most part the old—will prevent the development of the public-house in India. Is it not on the highroad to civilisation ?

Let us pass on to something older, more cheerful. Here is a shop which it is hard to classify. There is a basket platter of coarse flour, a lump of rock salt, an earthen *chatti* of clarified butter, a dish of curds, perhaps even another of *hulwa*, and a pile of *luddu*. So much for comestibles. For the rest there are hanks of coir rope, pipe stems and bowls, bells for cattle, a coil that is not rope but tobacco, nails, winnowing baskets, flour sieves, a plate of fresh dates for wedding presents, and last, not least, great skeins of *mangala*, the turmeric and vermilion dyed cotton which is tied round the bride's neck on the occasion of her marriage. Behind the counter, too, hung up by their lacquered bars, are the wedding stools which the bride takes with her to her husband's house.

And somewhere in the back premises lurk the lacquered wooden-bed legs, the decorated spinning wheels, even the round cowry-decked baskets that will also accompany her.

This shop, in fact, hardly appeals to the general public. It has its own particular *clientèle* whom

AN UNCLASSIFIED SHOP

.

●

it supplies with everything from birth to death,—
even with money; for the grey-haired jovial-look-
ing owner has no objection to—as it were—keep
the jewels of a family in safe custody in the iron
box with a marvellous native lock, of which he is
so inordinately proud, vowing it to be a hundred
times safer than Chubb or Bramah. He is ready
with everything which a Hindu home can possibly
require, and at the last will supply wood, oil, and
spices for the funeral pyre.

A step farther brings us to the cook-shop, where
you can see pulse puffs being fried in oil, and watch
the spitted *kababs* roasting over charcoal. Cold
curried vegetables, dough cakes, pickled carrots,
turnips and sugar, endless pilaus, and "double-
onioned" stews cater for both Hindus and Mahommedans, many of whom, being in various services,
and therefore away from their women kind, live
on such cook-shops, for the prices are marvellously
reasonable. It is a restaurant without any upkeep
save a fresh pile of *dhák* leaves every day.

Finally there is the *kobariya's* shop. The
dictionary gives the meaning of the word thus :—

"One who displays old things hung up on wide-
open doors."

Was there ever a better description? Old

things, and still older things, upside down, higgledy-
piggledy, hung on the top of each other: a
patent rat-trap shouldering a broken lamp, an
officer's tunic sheltering a pile of tent-pegs, a bazaar
pipkin on top of some priceless old plate, a parrot's
cage filled with French novels, a moth-eaten saddle
keeping company with an old sword. And over
all, sufficient scrap iron to furnish forth a foundry ;
and in an old cauldron, incense spoons, little brass
gods, prayer measures, sacred fire holders, all mixed
up with battered electroplated forks, hot-water
jug lids, and every conceivable kind of rubbish !

How two or three *kobariya's* shops would rejoice
the heart of the ladies who spend their time in
getting up rummage sales !

There are treasures to be found sometimes ; but,
on the other hand, there are unpleasant things to
be picked up, to say nothing of disease and death,
in the piles of old clothing which fill up the corners
from floor to ceiling.

When will some sensible Government issue an
edict by which all things that have been worn by
the dead shall be burnt or buried with the corpse,
as part of the outward husk which has to pass for
purification into inorganic dust ere it is fit again
to take its part in life ?

So, throughout the long length of the Indian bazaar, these shops repeat themselves again and again. Metal-workers, tin-smiths, butchers,—these often have a quarter to themselves. And, adown the street, the multi-colour crowd jostles and parts to let the newly wed or the dead pass through; while, in the balconies overhead, women, painted and tired, members of the oldest profession in the world, sit indifferent, drowsy, gazing with lack-lustre eyes at the life beneath them as if it were nothing.

A quail calls from its hooded cage. A municipal sweeper, coming along with his broom, propels an evil black flood along the gutter; and that tall, spare bronze-faced man in a white uniform who rides along at a foot's pace, his keen blue eyes everywhere, is the English police-officer.

He stops, says something to a yellow-legged orderly at his heels, then passes on.

Thereinafter there are tears in some balcony or liquor shop, since order must be preserved in the bazaar.

14

CHAPTER XI

PEOPLE speak of the art of India with bated breath, but the natives of that country have very little real artistic sense. On the slightest provocation they fly to aniline dyes; they prefer Manchester goods to their own beautiful hand-printed fabrics, and a Berlin-wool-work pattern will send them off at a tangent from the rhymed directions for making, let us say, an Irani carpet, which their fathers and grandfathers learnt and made, and which will remain for ever a thing of beauty.

And yet India is full of indigenous arts and crafts, and when untempted by the West these remain in many ways beautiful exceedingly.

In one way, however, all Indian art errs: it is too ornate. The tendency is to paint the lily, and gild refined gold. In nothing is this better seen than in the oldest known embroidery to be found

in India—that which is seen in what we call *phulkari* work.

The original was a somewhat sparse diapering in gold-coloured floss-silk on the madder-dyed native cloth, which by its coarse texture was peculiarly fitted for what is, really, a darning stitch. Its latest development—I mean, of course, before the European demand for cheap drapery ruined the work utterly—was practically the covering of a far finer fabric with silk of varying colours, leaving the substance of the stuff as a diaper; the effect being not nearly so good, and the production twice or three times as laborious. It is so in all things. Leisure has led India astray, and the bold, free decorations of a past age have been elaborated into minute if still beautiful adornment. So much in regard to form. In regard to colour Nature was kind, indeed, in the past. Before coal-tar was, the flora of India furnished forth infinite hues, soft, harmonious, each one of which, like the flowers from which they sprang, could hold their own in sunshine or in shade against a whole parterre of colour. These dye plants grow still, but they are ousted by what the natives call "bottle dyes." Bottle imps indeed—malevolent, destructive, which have but one good quality—

they are ephemeral. Even the grand old madder-
red, that standby of every Indian scene, which,
with the dull saffron yellow of the *dhâk* blossom
dye, blends with the biscuit-coloured background
of Upper India so marvellously, is fast disappear-
ing, its place taken by some metallic mixture
which does not need the labour of steeping the
cloth in oil and all the thousand and one separate
processes which made the dyeing of one woman's
veil in the old fashion the work of weeks. But
then I have such a veil which has been worn and
washed for over two hundred years, and is still a
glorious piece of colour, reminding one of the
russet and gold millet stalks amongst which it was
embroidered by some stalwart Jâtni woman.

Has this past gone for ever? I fear so. We
are not strong enough, we have not at heart a
sufficient enthusiasm for the perfection of beauty
—that is, not the beauty of form, of colour, of
cheapness only, but of durability and skilful-
ness, and usefulness also — to make it possible
for us to do as the Japanese Government has
done—that is, put the foot down—squash!—on
the production of cheap art for the European
market.

So, ere long, the Arts and Crafts of India will

be even as the arts and crafts of Manchester and Birmingham.

To consider them, even now, it is necessary to go back.

To begin with, the sculpture of India is very fine, very laborious.   One seldoms sees a *basso-relievo*; friezes and panels are very often in super-sensual relief.   In many cases the figures are absolutely detached from their background, in many more they are outlined by hollows deep enough to hold the whole depth of the image. For imagination they must surely take the first place in the world.   The so-called Hall-of-the-Four-Winds at Fattehpur Sikri, the marvellous arcade at Delhi, and the endless variety of column and capital, architrave and arch, in many a rock-cut temple, testify to the almost weird fancy of those who carved them.   To our modern modesty some of these imaginings must seem obscene, in-decent, but in the days when they were lovingly, reverently given shape from the rude stone, they were but common, everyday symbols of a great thought which the West has not, and which the East has almost forgotten.   Whether they shock our sensibilities or not, it is as well to remember that those who carved them carved with the whole-hearted reverence for mysterious truth which also guided the hands and tools of those who built our catacombs, our basilicas, our churches.

Taking architecture as the oldest Indian art of which there is any record, it is to be noted that stone is not supposed to have been used at all until after the invasion of India by Alexander the Great. It was the great King Asoka, however, who introduced it, as a means of preserving his rock and pillar cut edicts. For many centuries stone carving followed absolutely on the lines of wood building, the use of the arch being unknown until Mahommedan times. Immediately after this period, however, came the days of the Italian adventurer, who left his mark again on the architecture of India; so that altogether, sculpture in stone can scarcely be called indigenous. At the present day it is practically non-existent; but the older art of wood-carving remains, and scarcely a mud hovel is built without some rude attempt at decoration on the lintel.

The old Græco-Buddhistic marbles which he scattered over the north-west frontier are often very fine, many of the Gautamas especially being quite beautiful; but beyond a small colony of terra-

cotta workers in Lucknow there are practically now no modellers in India.

The oldest paintings in India are the frescoes at Ajunta. Their age is doubtful, but it is quite possible that they date from a century or two before Christ.

Judging by them, mural decoration did not advance at all during the years. Indeed, the frescoes to be seen nowadays on newly-built temples, or the houses with which money-lenders love to overtop their mud-hovel clients, are not to be compared with the old ones.

These modern productions are often extremely funny, especially when from excess of loyalty towards a legal system which enables *buniya-ji* to get his grip on the land he puts a *sahib* and a *mem-sahib* as supporters to his threshold. Temples nowadays run largely to extremely spidery pale-blue monkeys with excessively long tails. A picture of Kali Devi in her Terrific Form, with her tongue out, dripping blood, as she dances on her aggrieved consort Shiv', is also a favourite subject; for as the world grows old it favours the horrors which stimulates its jaded appetite. So, year by year, our newspapers become more and more hysterical, more and more ravening-as-wolves after garbage

and carrion ; and in India the ritual of religion, which
is to the people an amusement, as newspapers
are to us, becomes more and more full of incanta-
tions and charms, of small obscenities and puerile
superstitions. ✗ The priests go one better all round
in their effort to keep their hold on the people, and
the women, more idle than they used to be before
Manchester sent its cloths, and steam mills their
flour, go still one more, vying with each other in
the elaboration of ritual, till the *Stri achchar* or
woman's law has become a terror to mankind.

To revert to the art of painting.   Some quite
decent miniature work is done, and at Delhi the
descendants of the old court painters still make a
precarious living by portraits based on photography.
Some few years ago a slight stir was made in
Upper India by a purely native painter whose work
was curiously like that of the early Italian school.
One small picture, in particular, of a dead ascetic,
might easily have been taken for a Pieta.

Music is a difficult subject.   It is almost impossible for the Western ear even to imagine a
musical scale in which each tone is but an eighth
part of ours; yet India claims to be able to dis-
tinguish these infinitely trivial variations.

Of rhythm there is plenty; the insistent throb-

bing of a tom-tom gets on the nerves with its absolutely changeless accent; and there is melody of a sort. Of harmony, to our ears, none; and to harmonise a native tune is to treat it as FitzGerald treated the poor tentmaker, Omar Khayyam—that is, to translate it bodily into another world.

There are a few tunes to which the West can nod its head, feeling that it can assimilate or partially assimilate them—the eternal "*Taza-ba-Taza*" of the disreputable bazaar; "*Zachchmi*," an Afghan song beloved of native bands; last, but not least, "*Oh! Minnea Punnya*," the favourite of ayahs and nurseries.

But if the West is chary of accepting the music of the East, the East, as a rule, is chary of the Western music. "Home, sweet Home" (the first two bars of which is groaned out by almost every well-wheel in the land), "God save the King" (in devious variations), "Twinkle, twinkle, little Star," and the "Bluebells of Scotland" are the only tunes I have ever heard outside the Presidency towns. And for the most part, not the whole of them: three, or at most four bars, iterated and re-iterated, is quite enough.

Of musical instruments they have quite a number, the simplest, of course, being the drum

15

kettle or otherwise.   The little *doroo* or hour-glass-shaped drum, when twirled in the hand of an expert dancer, gives to her rhythmic movements just the *verve* and *élan* which the cachucha gains from the castanets.

The simplest of stringed instruments again is the *vina*, the oldest of all the many forms of guitar or lyre known to India.   It is held sacred to Krishna, who is the Eastern Apollo.   It has a sweet tinkling note, and is struck by a steel plectron. Then there are endless fiddles and violas, of which the *saringi* is the best known.   Wind instruments are few ; and yet if a native happen to have a cornet or a clarionet, he will, if he chance to be within a mile of you, make day and night hideous with, say, the first three bars of "God save the King"; for he is like the bullfinch,—the most "damnable iteration" distresses him not at all—his sense of rhythm is such that one phrase suffices—to him music hath neither beginning nor end !   But for real music India has as yet no ear.   Whether she will acquire one is doubtful.   She has solved the riddle of life to her own satisfaction by saying, "All is illusion"; and music lives by denying that illusion is possible.

One wonders vaguely what the Emperor Akbar's

"Song of the Hours" was like, when at dawn and eventide the choristers appeared bearing the twelve golden candlesticks, which they lit or extinguished with censings and scattering of rose leaves. It might have been so beautiful, it may have been mere screechings of horns and batterings of drums; but the ceremony at least wakes the imagination.

In the art of literature, India stands high. There is not much of it, but what there is, is good —some of it superlatively so. To write Sanskrit well requires real culture, yet most of the old speculative and scientific works are written in unimpeachable style. The later Mahommedan authors are over ornate, but a literature which can give us such incomparable books as the *Bhagavad-gita*, *Sakuntala*, the *Rubaiyat*, and *Babar's Memoirs* may well be content with itself.

So much for the arts of India.

Regarding the crafts, one stands arrested at once by the Indian workman's hand. What a marvel of subtle delicacy and supple strength it is! Simply to look at an Indian artisan's fingers is to see deft intertwining, swift knotting, a touch certain as the grave. By far the most wonderful sight I have seen in India was the sight of a lacquer-worker at Kasur engaged in engraving a little round lacquer box which I have now. It is an ordinary round *farash*-wood box, turned on a country lathe—that most simple and effective of tools—and thereinafter coated on the lathe with five successive layers of coloured lac—white, red, yellow, green, black. As a perfectly black box it lay in his hand. Then with one rapid turn of the lathe, the top, the side were grooved through to the green, the yellow, or the red, dividing the surfaces into circles or rings.

With this faint guide only, he began work with one rough graver, apparently made out of an old nail, and in a flash a marvellous floreated scroll-work began to appear. Down to the yellow for the curving lines, down to the green for intricate curved foliage, and then, with a sideways flourish, to the red, edged and spotted with yellow, for the flat surfaces of fruit or flowers. So the pattern of pomegranates and ~~dracæna~~ lilies grew, free, yet conventionalised to an accuracy of recurring outlines, true as a die ; an inner border of jasmine stars, cut clear to the white from the black, with fine yellow and red flourished scroll, an outer one of green zig-zagging on the black, and the box was handed to me by the maker, an absolutely illiterate man, with a deprecating smile. It was not worthy my honour's acceptance ; but I have it still, and as

I look at its perfect accuracy of sweeping curve, the extraordinary balance of the whole scheme of decoration which grew from one tool, I feel that the Indian artisan's hand is an asset of which we have not yet recognised the full value. Not that it will ever compete with machinery, if the machine-made perfection be our ideal.

Perhaps it is. At any rate, many of the old crafts of the Hindu are dying out. Some have already gone. The one old man who could still inlay crystal with gold is dead, and so, unless some curio-collector falls in love with the delicate hunting-scenes and flower-pieces on the little medallions that used to be set as waistbands, turban girdles, and such like, and by collecting them stimulates imitation, the last will have been heard of one very distinctive craft.

But, in truth, all the jewellery work of India is in danger of dissolution—if only because pure gold and silver is a necessity to it. Rough tools in a mere human hand cannot grapple with base alloy; that finds fitting moulder in a Nasmyth steam-hammer or a patent roller. And to-day, the richest of all Time's days, cannot afford the price of gold; scarcely the depreciated price of silver. So ornamentation comes from Birmingham or Berlin, and the precious metals are simply welded into rough fetters for wrist or ankle,—fetters which cost but a rupee or two for the making, and which serve as a savings bank to the wearer. Another thing which militates against the native jeweller is the lack of expert lapidaries. They cannot facet, and the day of table-cut gems is over,—though, indeed, for pure decorative effect few things could beat, for instance, the necklace of table emeralds which used, at any rate, to be a State jewel of the Nawabs of Bhawulpore. To see it worn over a light-brown brocade coat veiled with white muslin was like seeing the young green wheat-fields set in the salt - effloresced soil of the State to which it belonged.

And the pagoda-tree no longer thrives and bears fruit. So one sees no longer the great half-hoop rings of pearls, emeralds, sapphire diamonds, rubies, which on an Englishwoman's hand was as sure a guide to India—in the past or present—as an Englishman's yellow face was to an Indian liver.

The Chandni-Chowk at Delhi may seem to confute the stagnation in the jeweller's craft; but half the things one sees there are not really Indian-made. One thing is certain: it is becoming increasingly difficult to get an artificer in gold or

silver to work for you, as they used to do, at your own house.

The making of gold thread is a craft in itself, and as it is one which cannot be effectually imitated by a machine it is well worth while to watch it for once, say in Delhi, where it is carried to perfection by the descendants of the tinsel-makers of the Great Moghuls. The mere flattening of the parcel-gilt silver wire, fine as a hair, on a highly polished steel anvil, is an art in itself, but it is nothing to the manual dexterity required for the due casing of the silk thread with the tiny ribbon of gold. Yet all the tools required are a hook or ring a few feet above the floor, and a long-handled spindle. The silken thread, from a ball under the worker's feet as he squats on the ground, runs over the hook and is attached to the spindle. One rapid sweep of the latter along the worker's thigh sets it going, and both the slender supple hands are free, one for the thread, one for the reel of tinsel, which in a flash shoots upwards to arm's length, coiled like a snake about the spinning thread. A moment's arrest while the dexterous left hand twirls the made thread upon the spindle, and once more that rapid sweep along the thigh repeats a process of which it has been written "that it is doubtful whether any mechanical means could ensure such perfection or whether it could ever be attained by artisans unused to it."

Here then is evidence in favour of the hereditary craftsman, evidence which is not lacking where-ever we turn in India, but which is never more clearly seen than in some miserably poor high tenement house in Delhi as the sunlight and the gold tinsel together flash up the yellow silken thread, seeming to set it on fire.

The craft of weaving is another that is on the downward road in India, as elsewhere. It is inevit-able, of course, that this should be so. Spinning-jennies produce far more even thread than all but the most expert of human fingers; and even their production, though exquisite, can only be achieved by an expenditure of time and skill for which few care to pay in this hurried world of ours. Even in India the housewife prefers to sell the raw cotton for export, and buy her yarn for all but the very coarsest cloths. In truth, she prefers to buy the cloth ready-made. Yet still outside the walls of the towns, in open spaces within them, and nearly always on the outskirts of the villages, you may find the weavers'-walk, where, steering their long-handled spindles deftly in and out of the set-sticks, the weaver women twine the long warps, chattering shrilly as they go up and down, never pausing except under the greatest provocation, and then only with the spindles held taut on the thread.

But the provocation comes fairly often, since the weavers'-walk is a great gossiping ground, and half the scandal of the village is hatched there. It is a monotonous task laying webs, and requires enlivenment! The weaving of the finer qualities of Dacca muslin is an art in itself, as may be imagined from the fact that the yarn has to be spun during the short hour of light before the sunrise when the dew still be-diamonds the world and the air is moist. There are far fewer filaments of raw cotton in fine Dacca thread than in any machine-made yarn in the world, while its twist is about double; hence its extraordinary strength —a strength which enables a piece of muslin, fine as a cobweb, to stand a heavy embroidery of gold, and thereafter to bear much washing.

How some of the finer gold tissues with their raised flowers and intricate diaperings are made on the rude looms with bits of bamboo or grass for shuttles is a mystery. Once again, time and patience and long-inherited manual skill come to

16

take the place of brain. Such an expenditure of
pure labour would, with the British workman, who
requires four shillings a day at least for beef and
bread, place the product beyond the pale of
any one's purse, but with one who is content—ay!
better content than his European neighbour—to
work on half that sum a week, the production is
possible—nay, pleasurable; since work that is not
hurried work is great gain to humanity. There is
another softener of hard labour in India which does
not exist in England, and that is the dignity of
being recognised as a "great artificer." To be
pointed out as one possessed of unusual skill, as
the holder of secret recipes, as the inheritor of
acquired adaptations—or adaptability, it matters
little which,—all this is also great gain. To see
the smirk on the face of some old Mahommedan
zumlogi as he, and his fathers, and his little
loom are introduced to you by an admiring
populace as the best gold-tissue producers of
which the town boasts, is to learn that man does
not live by bread alone—still less by beef!

And this praise is not the property of weavers
or of any special trade. "So and so is a 'great
artificer'" stands to the credit of every one who
puts himself into his work. I have seen a gold

inlayer on steel, when shown a piece of work done by some unknown artist in such craft, salaam to it quite simply and say, "He was a workman indeed." Machinery and the division of labour render this attitude towards handicraft impossible in the West; but that is no reason why we should not admire it, and count it in the day's wage of the Indian craftsman. Perhaps we might rationally go one step farther, and hesitate ere we attempt to substitute for it one more ultimate sixpence.

To return to the crafts of India: that of the carpenter is remarkable for having been stationary for thousands of years. Joinery work is as rude to-day as it was, apparently, in Alexander's; and now, as then, the most beautiful carving conceivable is put on a casket or door-frame so badly dovetailed that it needs putty to hide deficiencies. This is, no doubt, largely due to the poverty of tools. The curiously set adze is, it is true, no mean substitute for a plane in the inherited hand of the Indian carpenter, when used on a wide surface; on a narrow one it is unreliable. The word inherited is used with intent; for, whether the adaptation or the adaptability of the muscles be handed on, certain it is that the ten-year-old son of an Indian carpenter will use his father's adze with an accuracy, a certainty, which no grown man of another trade can compass without years of training.

But it is hopeless to go down the list of Indian crafts; there are so many, and they all depend so much on the personal equation, which is the outcome of countless generations of experience in that particular work *and no other*. The man who vaguely seeks "employment" in the West, who has been a butcher, been a candlestick-maker, and is quite ready to try his hand at plastering or hay-making, is an unknown quantity in India—at present. That this close guildship in trades does away with competition is true; but then competition brings with it so many evils, not the least of these being the craving for novelty. The wares of an Indian potter have served their purpose for centuries. The potter himself, with their every curve hidden in his pliant thumb, has no temptation to vary their shape into the hideous contortions to be seen in our china shops. In decoration also he is hedged about in every cell of body and mind, not by the experience of one life only, but of many lives. And so—and so the only monstrosities in Indian arts or crafts are those due directly to alien buyers or alien teachers.

It is almost incredible, the truly terrible teaching that is given at times with the very best intentions. For how much hideous broché-stitch worked into rainbow-hued comforters are not our mission ladies responsible? and what fiend in human shape presented the beautiful Damascene workers in gold and steel of Sialkot with the pattern of an ink-stand—an apple on a vine leaf—round which one enterprising artist had inscribed in a scroll, "God bless Master-sahib Esquire Bahadur"?

Such things are not for laughter: they are for tears. Yet for some of the old handicrafts of India there seems to be no place left in the twentieth-century world.   Take, for instance, the Kashmir shawl industry. So many shawls come from India to England every year as tribute; and legend has it that one of these went to every bride about the court of that gracious lady, Queen Victoria.   For the rest, who needs or buys them, except here and there a chance rajah or nawab? So, nowadays, even in Kashmir, one seldom happens on a shawl-working family; yet it is a picture whose loss is to be regretted.

A deep thatch giving shade to the worker's eyes, light to his fingers; a warp of threads wide as the shawl itself; and huddled against this—the children

perhaps given a bit of plain grounding—a whole
family of sorts and sizes, all bending over their
bundles of tiny bobbins, deftly weaving them in
and out, as with unerring sequence Grandfather,
his back against the brick pilaster, his pipe beside
him, drones out the pattern,—so many black, one
white, two yellow, a green, fourteen red, and so on
all along the line.   A bright little maid of ten, a
greasy little red cap perched on her black pig-tails,
watches eagerly for her turn, and is at work almost
before the old man has sung out "twe-en-ty green."
For it is a green shawl set thick with the pines
whose shape is taken from the winding curves of
the river which flows at the workers' feet.

How does the old man remember each line of
the pattern, not in one Kashmir shawl, but in
many ?

That is a secret—the secret of Weissman's
kaim plasma !

CHAPTER XII

PRACTICALLY this is the India which the globe-trotter comes to see, and he goes away with a hod of bricks and mortar on his back, which he is destined to carry with him in all his recollections of that country.

But the real beauty of India lies in the fact that, relatively to its population, there is hardly a building in it at all. You may travel through miles on miles of country without coming upon any more solid sign of human inhabitancy than a reed hovel or a mud hut.

In Bombay, of course, there are buildings—beautiful buildings, reminiscent for the most part of kindergarten toys and a cheap Glasgow emporium. Then there is Fattehpur Sikri, that dream in red sandstone. They are poles asunder, these two towns, yet they pivot the whole round world of India — its past of regrets, its present of progress.

In most large Indian cities nowadays stand representatives of both factors. There is a town hall, or an institute, or a museum of some sort, showing, for the most part, exactly the extent to which the genius of the East has permeated the mind of its Western designer. Sometimes there is a far-off echo of the tune of the tombs about it; sometimes it is frankly Renaissance, with a minaret or two superadded as a sop to its surroundings. Then, somewhere, hidden away perhaps in a narrow dark lane, or forgotten among outside ruins amongst twisted *Jhund* or *babool* trees, there will be a tomb or a temple telling us of the past.

There are a few places in India still, however, in which one can forget the present, where—if one can only get rid of fellow-passengers, guides, and such like—one can realise what that past India must have been.

Such are Amber, Oodeypore, Fattehpur Sikri, and, in a lesser degree, the ruins of old Delhi; for in such places as the Caves of Elephants, the Tope at Sanchi, the rock-cut temples at Ajunta, and Ellora, the mind is too full of the sight to be seen, of the marvellous ingenuity of the cutters and

builders, for us to dream of the scenes which have been enacted with the building as a background.

But these others are different.   In Amber, perched high on the Rajputana hills, one can see the flower of chivalry riding up the stone-set slopes, and hear the clash of arms resounding through the Hall of Audience.   It is a fine place, Amber.   Compared with modern Jeypore, with its horrible Albert Hall and the still more appalling motto "Welcome" in gigantic white letters on its rocky hill, with its so-called "Palace of the Winds," built of an intolerable pale pink stucco of which any honest, self-respecting sou'wester would make mincemeat in a moment, Amber is rest and peace.   The mere sight of it, a city of the dead, sleeping beside the little cool lake set in the glare of the red Rajputana rocks, makes one forget the soulless city of the living, one has left behind one.

Up the steep stone stairs one climbs into the great Hall of Audience, with its quaint stuccoed pilasters hiding the finest carving in India beneath its smug mask of mediocrity.   This was done in the Emperor Jehangir's time, who, sending emissaries to command the instant destruction of a building said to eclipse all Moghul efforts after magnificence,

17

received them back again to learn that they had
spared a hall of whose beauty the Emperor had
heard a grossly exaggerated account, and which
was not worthy of his anger. That was many
hundred years ago, but the stucco remains.

There is something very beautiful about the
women's apartments at Amber—something which
makes one see the proud innermost soul of the
Rajputni who would die rather 'than surrender
herself to the lightest touch of a conqueror; or,
prouder still, resent the least suspicion of familiarity
on the part even of their own men. The story is
still told of the Kohan princess who, amid the
luxury and depravity of a later court, clung to the
old flowing petticoat of the Rajput race, and who,
when, half in desire to see her dressed in the
scantier fashion of other court ladies, half in banter,
her husband caught up a pair of scissors and vowed
he would curtail her draperies, seized his sword
and told him fiercely that such a jest was ill-timed,
and that if he repeated it he would find that a
sword in the hand of a Kohan woman was a better
weapon than scissors in the hand of a Jeypore
man. There is something very fine in the passion
and poetry, the reserve and right-thinking, of these
women, who must have swept over these marble

floors so often, decked like a bride to meet their conquering lord, decked like a bride to meet his dead body and burn with it on the funeral pyre.

Surely some of them, looking through the fretted marble lattices upon the wild hills, and seeing the freedom of the birds of the air, which even now wheel and swoop restlessly over the valley of ruins, as if they saw some quarry amongst the bare rocks, must have longed for the wings of a hawk, so that they might fly away and be at war with their husbands, their lovers, in some distant field of fight.

One can imagine them, waiting, and watching, and wondering what fate held in store for them, as they sat looking out from the balcony over the still reflections in the still lake to the broken ridges of red hills far away beyond the yellow wastes of sand from which rise the rocks of Rajputana.

Ay! as one sits in the shadow feeling drowsy and dreamful by reason of the glare and blare of the yellow sunlight on hot stone, one can almost credit the old legend which tells how the Princess Beautiful, besieged to war's-point by chieftain lovers, seeing her unhappy country distraught by her all-innocent charms, sent a message bidding the many disputants cease quarrelling and come to a wedding feast, at which she would choose her fate. And when they came, lo! the first gift uncovered, of all the honourable gifts that lay before the guests, was a Beautiful Head, holding between its closed, kissable lips the message that they had chosen Death for the bridegroom.

"Si non e vero e' ben trovato"; for it breathes the very spirit of the Rajputni.

That breathes through Oodeypore also, where a woman now holds the headship of every Rajput in India. It has a stirring history, this little principality of Mewar, of which Chitore was once the capital. The town stands now, half-rock, half-fortress, rising high above the broken ground where so many besieging armies have camped, and where history tells us of at least three desperate sorties when the last hope of holding out was gone. One passes Chitore now in the train, a sullen purple shadow when seen against a primrose dawn.

Who sees it thus—remembering those three awful days when the flaming banner of the sun (a golden disc on a round shield of black ostrich feathers) led the flood-tide of Rajput chivalry dressed in the yellow robes of sacrifices to certain death, while the flames of the women's funeral pyres rose up behind them—may well dream that

on the battlements there stands the figure of the King's herald, clad in his white robes, and with his silver sword proclaiming to all time that the Rajputs were indeed as their name implies, the Sons of Kings.

Then there is old Delhi, or, rather to be accurate, Indrapastha, since the name Dilli was not known until a century or so before Christ. What strikes one there is the vast extent of what one may call formless, foundational ruin—mere heaps of broken brick, the angle corner of a wall, a mound that was perchance once a gateway. It is not much to look at, but seen under a lowering, rain-burdened December sky it is suggestive beyond words,—the wide rolling purpling plain broken by these waves of ruins into the semblance of a vast sea, sullen, mysterious, with the great shaft of the Kutb rising like the mast of some sunken galleon, and here and there—half submerged, like a wreck upon the rocks—the shadowy darkness of a ruined palace or a tomb of dead kings. From the iron pillar—the "arm or weapon of victory"—which is ascribed to Raja Dhava in the fourth century before Christ, and which is buried so deep in the earth that but one-half of its total length is visible, through the monolith of the great King Asoka, who lived in the third century, onwards through many a forgotten tomb, to the marvellous spire of the Kutb built by the Slave King; past that to the mound-like pile of the Taghluk fort, and so to the almost perfect buildings of the Moghul times,—we have here a record of many centuries, of seven cities, spread before us for eleven long miles. There is nothing like it in the world.

And submerged utterly by the ocean of earth, there must lie here the vestiges of still further generations, of the aboriginal chieftains, and the great Snake Kings, the richest in the world in jewels, gold, and women. There is something very dream-compelling about the thought of these passionate, luxurious, serpent-worshipping people, who flung gold away like water, and let a woman's kiss lure them from even kingship.

Here but three miles from the gates of modern Delhi stands the tomb of Humayun, beautiful exceedingly in itself, with its marvellous arches which spring upwards with all the glad litheness of a rising skylark, but which has gained another significance from being the place where Hodson of Hodson's Horse laid peremptory hands on the foolish Bahadur Singh, last of all the Moghuls, and brought him and his scheming wife back by threats and promises to Delhi, there to be tried for his life, and convicted to something worse than death— unending exile. It is a fine, yet a pitiable story, —the fire and dash of the young cavalry officer whose grip had for weeks been tightening round the doomed King, his almost solitary venture into danger; for the King in flight and hiding had yet with him many hundreds of loyal followers.

One can see the little procession, as Hodson describes it himself, making its way that 21st of September, he himself riding beside the Queen's litter.

So far good; but what is to be said of that second procession on the following morning when he escorted the Princes, lured by promises which he knew he could not perform ?

So much controversy has raged round this point as to whether Hodson was or was not justified in what he did, that it is useless further to discuss it. But one thing may be mentioned to prove indisput- ably that it could not have been either surprise or attack which made Hodson give the order to shoot the Princes: Prince Aboolbakr was wearing a talisman round his wrist, and Hodson's orderly *made him take it off* before he shot him.   That is

from the orderly's own lips, and it does not look
like a sudden alarm.

Close by Humayun's tomb is the mosque and
observatory whence the Emperor fell, interrupted
in his star-gazing by the call of the muazzim to
prayer. They were all fond of the stars, those
three great Moghuls, Babar, Humayun, Akbar, and
Babar was, amongst many other things, no mean
astronomer for the times.

Of Delhi itself there is small need to speak,
except in regard to the great Mutiny of 1857, of
which later on. Even its palace, home once of the
famous peacock throne, is dominated by the Ridge,
red still as if with the blood that was spilt on it.
The Jumna Masjid, itself dignified by a majesty of
its own, as it stands supreme on its many-stepped
plinth of red sandstone, yields to the simple tablet
in the old arsenal, which tells the nine names of
the nine heroes who fired the mine.

And yet the Diwani-khas at Delhi comes next
to the Taj Mahal in beauty of proportion. Shah
Jehan—great-great-grandson of our jack-of-all-
trades, who was yet master of many, Babar—must
have inherited his ancestor's keen artistic sense,
for whatever he built was beautiful. That he
employed Italian architects does not affect the fact

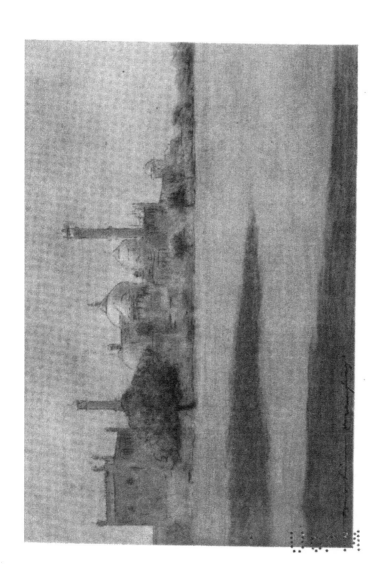

that he employed good ones, and only approved such plans as pleased his sense of form and colour.

There are few things in the world more soul-satisfying than to stand, as you come from the King's bath, in one of the outer archways of the Private Hall of Audience, and look down through its pillared arcades to the great yellow triptych of blazing sunlight beyond, in which the white marble traceries of the King's pleasure-house show like a bridal veil, while through the aisles a chastened light filters from the gardens full of pomegranates and peaches.

But in all these places the mind has freedom to wander and choose its subject through the centuries. In Fattehpur Sikri all thought is centred round one man—the man who built it, who lived in it, who in a way deserted it when years had brought him disillusionment. For Akbar was not one to be satisfied with the outward show of kingship, and power, and influence. He was a man of very strong affections; his son was a disappointment to him, and the murder—the needless murder by that son—of Abulfazl, the Emperor's dearest friend, his almost brother, was an abiding grief.

For all that, Fattehpur Sikri holds the best of Akbar; and that, briefly, is the best of India, for

18

she has produced no man like unto him. He laid the foundation-stone of the city when he and his wife, a Hindu princess of the house of Jodhpore, in bitter grief over the loss of their twin boys, went to live for a time beside the hermitage of the saint Salim Chisti, in pursuance of a vow. Here he built a palace, and here nine months afterwards Prince Salim, so called after the saint, was born. Here also he was brought up. So every stone of Fattehpur Sikri represents Akbar's fatherhood, his hope that a son would come after him whose hands would be strong enough to hold the reins of government. He dreamt of the future, and his dream remains cut in red sandstone. Such a solid dream too! Simple, and solid, and strong, with the exception of Raja Birbal's house, which he, the Prime Minister, built for his daughter; for Birbal had had enough of wives! Cynical, worldly, Epicurean, the stories they tell of him to this day in India show him a man of culture, possessing the wisdom of the serpent, inclined at heart to jest bitterly over the riddle of life which he could not understand.

And so, in the middle of all Akbar's wide court-yards and aspiring arches, Birbal's house stands, overlaid with ornament, capricious utterly, sur-

charged with the spirit of "let us eat and drink, for to-morrow we die."

Such was not Akbar's thought. One can almost see the man, as he may have stood many a time, looking out through his Gateway of Victory—the finest commemorative archway in the world, beside which the arches of Trajan or Constantine fade into insignificance — looking out over the wide expanse of India, stretching from his feet to the horizon of land and sky, and wondering what was to come after him.

Perhaps his eyes may have often travelled to the sweeping, upspringing arch soaring away above his head, and lingered on the words chiselled round it in undying stone :

Said Jesus, on whom be peace! "This world is a bridge.
"Pass over it, but build no house there. Who hopes for an hour hopes for eternity. The rest is unseen."

There is scarcely any one who has given a more outward and visible form to his inward and spiritual life than Akbar. The routine of his court was one long tale of symbolism. Who but he would ever have thought of coining the immortal money— those marvellous gold pieces with a tulip or a rose stamped on one side, and on the other the simple legend "God is greatest"? Except, indeed, upon

the one called the Henseh, that almost fantastic
square of gold worth nearly two hundred pounds,
on which this warning showed :

This coin is for the necessities of those who travel on the
road to God.

That was the keynote of the immortal money.
No ultimate sixpence for pleasure, or luxury, or
wealth ; only something to supply bread and the
more than bread by which man lives as he passes
over the Bridge of Life.

The symbolism of that nightmare of beauty the
Panch-Mahal, quaint superstructure on superstructure of pink and yellow sandstone which
stands not far from Birbal's house overlooking the
women's apartments and gardens, has been forgotten nowadays, and men puzzle over its purpose.
What was it, with its tier on tier of open arcading,
through which every wind of heaven may blow?
An old Mahommedan told me—and the idea grows
upon one as the character of Akbar stands out more
intensely romantic, imaginative, original, the more
one reads of him—that the Emperor built it as a
playground for that darling of his heart, that apple
of his eye, the Prince Salim. On wet days the
heir to India and the future was not to be " cribbed,

cabined, confined." He was to have shelter, but with the wide diversity of God's earth in it. No recurring line, no stereotyped curve, was to lead his young mind into the groove which breeds intoler- ance, and so every tier of building is different, and no two columns are alike. To stand on the second story surrounded by thirty-and-five shafts and capitals, each one differing from the other, is almost like standing in the vaulted aisles of a forest. Yes! I think my old Mahommedan was right. The story fits square into the square blank.

One cannot leave Fattehpur Sikri without paus- ing awhile in the Argument House, or, as some prefer to call it, the Hall of the Privy Council. It is by far the most original thing in the whole of Akbar's city, it springs direct from Akbar's most unfettered mind. It is fairly large, fairly lofty, vaulted into a central cusp, below which there rises from the floor to the height of ten or twelve feet an enormous column of red sandstone, the capital of which, highly decorated and set round with a carven balustrade, forms a sort of throne. From the four corners of the room, which are cut off into galleries, sweep out four low wide arches to meet this central throne. Balustraded in like manner, they give means of access to it. Thus we have, as it were, a two-storied building with no floor between the stories. Here in the centre, alone, unsupported by the echoing flattery which surrounds most Eastern kings, Akbar used to sit, watching, listening, while from the four galleries the voices of the disputants rose, and below him—yawning, no doubt, over the, to them, tedious entertainment—sat his court.

Sometimes, we are told, if the King wearied, he would slip away, leaving the learned men wrangling before emptiness; but more often he would sit through to the bitter end, enjoying, so they say, the success of every skilled debater, no matter of what caste or creed. Here the Jesuit fathers Acquaviva and Anthony Monserrat held up the flag for Christianity against all the learned Mahommedan preachers and Hindu pundits of the day.

Did Akbar favour any of the creeds, the dogmas, which he thus heard expounded? It is hard to say. One thing is certain: in his own personal life he showed the asceticism of the Hindu sadhu, the grip and go of the Mahommedan zealot, the patience and loving-kindness of the Christian. For the rest let us leave him, as we have imagined him, standing under his Arch of Victory, looking out

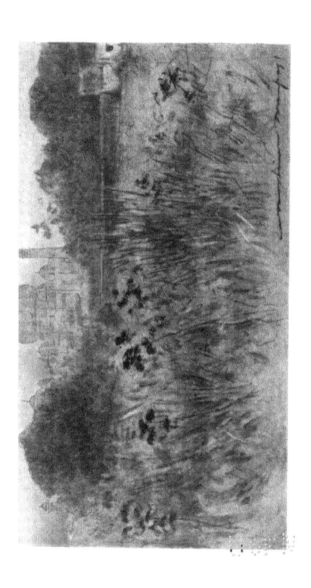

over the world he had conquered, with these words
over him :

The rest is unseen.

To turn to the other buildings which are worth
seeing in India.

A great deal has been said in praise of the Pearl
Mosque at Agra. It is delicate and pure, superlatively. It is like some beautiful novice dedicated
in her innocence to be the Spouse of the Church ;
but it is no more. It cannot appeal to the work-
worn, world-worn souls of men as do the wide
echoing spaces of the Black Mosque at Delhi.
The tomb of Jehangir at Lahore, Wazir Khan's
Mosque, and in a lesser degree the Jumna Masjid
at Delhi—which should be seen empty, by moonlight—have each and all a real soul of beauty.

And what is to be said of the Taj Mahal ? Only
this—that it rejoices the heart to think that in his
long, sad years of blindness its builder Shah Jehan
must have had the memory of its unearthly beauty
as a consolation. To know, that for once you have
nigh touched perfection, is great gain.

For the rest, I saw the Taj for the first time
when I was leaving India after five-and-twenty
years of residence therein. I was prepared to
criticise. I had heard so much of its beauty that

I was inclined to doubt it. And my verdict—of value simply as a personal equation—is that it is a bit of the New Jerusalem. It neither requires moonlight nor sunset; it brings its own atmosphere, its own light that "never yet was on sea or shore."

And, surely, of all the quaintly upside down, blindingly contradictory things in the wide world is this, that in the land of Great Moghuls, Grand Turks, harems, zenanas, down-trodden womanhood, loveless marriages, polygamy, bestial couplings, and so forth—*vide* the reports of many excellent, well-intentioned men and women—this monument of exceeding, unparalleled beauty should stand, as one of the Seven Wonders of the World, a record of the love given to a wife who died when her thirteenth child was born!

CHAPTER XIII

THE TEMPLES OF INDIA

CONSIDERING how temples abound in India, and considering that each sight-seer who looks at them has, as a rule, two eyes, it is surprising how few people realise either what a temple is, or what the worship is which the priests conduct in them.

Those who do grasp the foundational facts are chiefly missionaries, and they condemn root and branch a system and ritual which at first sight— and, indeed, very often at last sight also—seems utterly unspiritual.

Indian temples, then, are not really temples in the sense in which churches can be called God's temples. They are simply shrines; shelter, that is, for the image of a god or godling. They are the receiving houses for the tithes set apart as a remembrance of things spiritual.

A good Hindu need never go near a temple

He can pay his due through a servant's hand if he chooses. If he does go, he will simply present his offering, salaam to the symbol within, and go away. He has sought and he receives no spiritual refreshment. He has acknowledged something beyond and above his ordinary life with which it is expedient to keep in touch. The very ignorant, no doubt, believe that they can get at the ear of this Something; but the native of India is not the only person in the world who cherishes this belief. They do not all offer sugar cups and curded milk; but they offer what they presume pleases the great Power more than corporeal gifts.

All the ritual of Christianity has for its aim the realisation by man of his unity with God. Our beautiful English Liturgy is instinct with this desire. To the Hindu this fact is undoubted. He knows himself only as something which after long ages will return whence it came; to what— from want of not words, but ideas—he is forced to call absolute nothingness, because in his present state of development it is unthinkable. It is not therefore necessary for the good Hindu to seek help in the realisation of his oneness with his Creator. He simply acknowledges the fact by treating that Creator as if He were very man. He

builds Him a house and gives tribute to the priests
to keep Him comfortable, and duly supplied with
all things which are desirable to mere man.

Having done this, there is no doubt that many
go no further; but the spiritually minded begin
religion when they leave the temple, having given
tithes of mint and cummin.

And yet, even so, there can be no question that
—almost ignored as it is by most writers, even
so generally fair a one as W. J. Wilkins—the
reverent drinking of the *Charan amrit* or "water
of life," that is, the water in which the god's feet
have been bathed, is a sort of a sacrament. It is
supposed to confer some spiritual good on the
soul of the drinker; at least, this is my experience.
"If you will come here, my daughter, to the
temple to-morrow at dawn," an old Brahman has
said to me, "I will give you *Charan amrit*, and
then you will become a real Hindu." This was at
Benares; and, had I gone, I have no doubt I
should have been mulcted of five rupees! But
the idea was there! Indeed, the mere derivation
of the word "amrit" or "a'mirt," which is the
Sanskrit death with the negative affixed, by showing it to be the "Elixir of Life" shows its sacra-
mental meaning. I have known Hindu widows

who found exactly the same comfort in a daily drinking of it as many a Christian woman does in daily communion. It is not always drunk at the temple; it is often taken home and used as holy water.

The ritual of the temple is, as a rule, confined to the Brahmans; but in Benares about dawn the temple ways are literally thronged with women, each bearing a quaint little brass cruet-stand, holder of sandal-wood powder, rice, ghi, curds, and sugar, whilst hanging from the other hand will be a jasmine or marigold chaplet.

They are going to attend "The Uprising," when the Brahmans, muttering texts the while—what texts it is impossible to say,—take the deity of the shrine from its bed, wash it, anoint it with oil, and return it to its proper seat for the day.

The ritual of this is so complex, it involves so many changes of posture and genuflexions, the employment of so many acolytes and accessories, that seeing it only from a distance, performed in the always dark and generally overcrowded inner shrine, it is impossible to grasp what is going on; but I remember that the first time I watched it I was irresistibly reminded, in the swift precision of the celebrants, their nasal twang, the celerity

with which they changed the *venue*, and their absolute lack of all reverence in look or manner, of a baptism I once saw in Milan Cathedral, when a blue-chinned sensual-looking priest christened three babies, changing his stole and kissing it, juggling with oil and salt and bottles the while, in an incredibly short space of time. Sacerdotalism is inevitably the same all over the world. The constant familiarity breeds, not contempt, but a curious indifference.

The whole worship of the shrine consists in attending to the idol as if it were a man or woman and apportioning its days with propriety. There are, in all, seven ceremonies, the chief of these being "The Uprising," "The King's Feast" or dinner, "The Joining" or the celebration of the meeting of Day and Night at sunset. For underneath all the thirty thousand little godlings lurks the one worship of the sun as the Light of Life.

The texts and the ritual vary somewhat day by day, but how or wherefore it is impossible to say; "it has always been so" or "the priests know" being the answer to all inquiries.

There is no reason to doubt the former statement, and therefore we are at liberty to suppose that the same anthropomorphic ritual that now

obtains was the worship in the old Brahmanical
rock temples. In using the word anthropomorphic,
however, it must be remembered that the native
of India does not make his God in the likeness of
man because he can conceive of nothing that is
not man, but because he recognises that he himself is part of that mysterious Something outside
and beyond him which it is impossible for him to
reduce to terms except as man.

As in all other things, however, the actual and
the theoretical differ widely in temple worship.
The almost incredible rapacity of the priests, the
gullibility of the women, are beyond words. The
rapacity grows, too, with the growing years, as one
by one the Brahman's richer, better educated
clients break away from his authority. As the
keeper of a shrine said to me mournfully, " Nowadays the pilgrims deduct ' third-class tikkut ' from
their offerings and I starve."

Naturally ; and this is a grievance that will
increase. The pilgrimage to Benares, for instance,
is a favourite one with widows, but they are
literally not safe without some strong protector.
With the Ganges at hand a stray widow or two
can easily be dispensed with, after her money has
been secured by intimidation. I heard terrible

tales of things that had really happened from four widows, who implored me to take a Cook's tourist party of them down with me when the great eclipse fair was on. They had no men folk, they said, and they dared not go alone.

In truth, one can well imagine the helplessness of that most helpless of God's creatures, an Indian woman who has been sheltered since she was born, in the little dark purlieus and tortuous lanes which fill up the space between the Temple of *biseshwar* and the river at Benares.

And yet how perfect they are—as a picture—those high, windowless walls, pale ochre, flesh-colour, purple, a niche here, a niche there, dripping with the oil of many votive lamp-lets; yet with nothing in them to be worshipped, maybe, except a worn stone, the print perhaps of a blood-red hand.

A door in the wall, just an ordinary square door, low, rudely carved, but———Ye powers above! what a glimpse through it!

A wide cloister, a spired shrine, a motley crowd, coloured, garlanded, the clang of a great brazen bell, and over all a chanting voice and a smell of incense, the whole set round with three high, almost windowless walls; above them more spires rising into the sky, that seems pale with the very excess of light.

Here, almost blocking the narrow lane, sits a seller of garlands. There is a platter of white purple reflexed datura blossoms among his wares— such deadly-looking flowers, holding such an un-kenned sweetness with a hint of poison in it. A veiled woman buys one, a pice clinks on the plate ; she hurries away towards the Great God's temple. What is she going to beg of Shiva-jee ? Who knows ? Something secret, for the datura is the flower of death.

There, causelessly, a mere hole cut in the wall and arched over, is a relic-vendor's shop. He has the quaintest things on sale, and the bands of pilgrims as they pass, close-herded by priests and guides, have to stop, in obedience to covert nods and winks of the shopkeeper and his touts, to over-haul the stock-in-trade. See! there is a priceless *saligrama* (it is only the glass ball from a soda-water bottle)—What! not give eight annas for it ? Then take it, and good luck, for four, and bless the good priests who brought them to an honest man ! The tall country bumpkin, in charge of his long tail of womenkind, pulls out four annas sheepishly, and the glass soda-water ball goes off

to be cosseted, and anointed with oil, and powdered with sandal-wood or red vermilion in some Hindu household. Women will tell their worries and troubles to it; perhaps it may be held before some one's dying eyes; it may even perform miracles. Who can tell?

Not all customers are so easy to please, however, and I once gauged the fierce, fanatical, blind rage of this temple-quarter of Benares by refusing to pay five rupees for a *saligrama* which had a violet tinge. I did not wish, I said, to buy a vindictive avatar. The seller flung the sacred thing back among its cheaper comrades with muttered curses, and as I moved on amid dark looks I heard the remark "The *Ml'echcha* knows too much," in a tone which suggested a desire to teach me that a little knowledge is a dangerous thing.

About *biseshwar* itself, that small, absolutely-dark recessed square beneath the chased gold spire, there is a curious air of mystery that filters out into the alley which encircles it.

What lies inside the low door? One gains through a hole in the wall a glimpse of deep obscurity, of bending figures lit up by a flickering lamp, a floor covered with garlands. There is a very ancient *lingam*, I am told—a pillared stone

20

of polished black marble. That is all. But it is
jealously guarded. My Hindu widow promised to
take me inside, and an old and very holy Brahman
offered to do the same; but it was not worth it.
Besides, knowledge would have spoilt the mind-
picture of the golden spires, the half-carven, half-
crumbling temple, the intense shadow in the alley,
the careless crowding in of flower-laden worshippers
going where I may not, cannot go. Their faces
are full of eager hope and reverence; they believe
in something of which I know naught, have a
security that is far from me. I am outcast.

Outcast in the streets of Benares! What a
fate for gods or men! where every other shop sells
a chaplet or *Ram-dakkan*, shaped like a carpenter's
square, with "Ram-ram, ram-ram" running round
endlessly appliqued in blue cloth on red, or red on
blue, in which the faithful hand can rest and count
its rosary unseen, without letting the right hand
know what the left hand is doing! No, Benares
is no place for the *Ml'echcha.* And yet he must
remember it always with reverence. To see it
once from the river-bank at the early dawn-tide of
some great festival is to understand once and for
all the power which, certainly for three thousand
years, has kept India absolutely unprogressive.

As she was in the days of Megasthenes or Arrian, so she was when I first knew her.

The secret of this stability lies open to the world, challenging the light of a new day, on the ghauts at Benares.

This world, even the city itself, is illusion; true life lies behind it and all earthly things. Why struggle for personal comfort to the personal passing body. Keep it pure, undefiled. That is the whole duty of man.

In this search for purity every thought of the vast crowd of bathers is centred, and it lingers still in the half-charred bodies of the dead which sweep down the rushing yellow tide of the river towards the unseen sea.

CHAPTER XIV

THE WOMEN OF INDIA

THIS is an extremely difficult subject of which to treat fairly, chiefly because it is impossible to swallow wholesale the two opposing estimates of Indian womanhood—the one favoured by most Anglo-Indians and fostered by missionary reports, which represents it as being thoroughly degraded, hopelessly, helplessly depraved, and utterly enslaved; the other—of late so enthusiastically preached by Miss Margaret Noble in her book *The Web of Indian Life*—which asserts that, on the contrary, the ideals of the Indian woman are the highest in the world, and that her conduct is an example, her life free and happy.

Naturally, it is difficult to bring these two absolutely genuine beliefs into line, especially if we adopt the Western standpoint and begin by asserting that happiness must hold hands with freedom.

The only thing to be done is to take the assertions bit by bit, and see if they are borne out by facts.

Let us therefore begin with the ideal. In the West we formulate as our ideal woman a human being of equal rights with man; mistress of her own sex, as he is master of his; therefore free to use that sex as she chooses. Mother *in posse*, she has *in esse* a right to refuse motherhood. She has therefore the right to go down to the grave still withholding from the world its immortality, still denying to it vast possibilities. For it must not be forgotten that to every woman in the world the Angel of the Annunciation brings the divine message, proclaiming that of her, perchance, a saviour shall be born. For the greatest poet, painter, musician, statesman, teacher, remain still amongst those unborn.

In the East this is not so. The ideal there, is of a human being who is not the equal of man; who cannot be so, since the man and the woman together make the perfect human being to whose guardianship is entrusted the immortality of the race. Outside marriage there should be no sex, and not to marry is wilfully to murder the possibility of life.

That is one point of divergence. The next shows even greater cleavage. The Western woman is taught that she has the right to monopolise the whole body and soul of a man. She can demand his love—that mysterious something over and above duty, over and above mere sexual attraction or friendship, which is the sole sanctifier of marriage.

The ideal Eastern woman knows nothing of monopoly or love. The sole sanctifier of her union with a man is the resulting child; the sole tie, the tie of fatherhood and motherhood. Therefore if she has no children she has two courses open to her: either she must bring a more fortunate handmaiden to her lord, and cherish the children as her own; or she must yield her place in hearth and home, in prayer and offering, give up her spiritual union with her husband, and live apart. Marriage to her, as to her husband, is no personal pleasure: it is a duty to the unborn—a duty which involves self-restraint on both,—on her, since she has voluntarily to give up any personal right on her sex; on the man, because he also has to yield his liberty, since the woman who hands on his immortality is as his mother, and must be treated with absolute respect.

Now there can be no question as to which of these two ideals claims the greatest amount of self-abnegation. Undoubtedly the Eastern.

In other ways also the Eastern outlook on life demands more moral courage. The Western girl is taught that what is sauce for the goose is sauce for the gander; the Eastern girl is taught that this is not so. Her chastity, for instance, is of infinitely greater importance to the home than is the man's, and she accepts the undeniable fact; and by doing so recognises the supreme importance of her own position.

Before passing on to practice, it will be instructive to consider how flatly Western law denies the attitude of the Western woman towards marriage. She proclaims that unless she can find divine love, marriage is no marriage; it asserts that she may love whom she chooses, provided the sexual relationship with her husband remains unimpaired. The husband cannot object to her failure to be to him companion, helpmeet, friend; he cannot even complain if she refuses to be a mother. She may neglect his house, his children, play skittles with his money, his reputation. She stands immune from interference on the rock of her sex; all the rest is mere talk.

This curious antagonism between faith and works makes her position oddly undefined. Like a shuttlecock she bandies, and is bandied over the network of sex which constitutes modern society, claiming a point here, repudiating it there, clinging to the bat of marital faithfulness with one hand, with the other wielding the doctrine of spiritual affinities, until it is no wonder that the Divorce Court is full. Lucky is it that in normally healthy cases love follows on marriage, else we should require more judges, more courts!

To come now to practice. It may be conceded at once that the Indian woman falls further from her ideal than the Western one; but then her ideal is higher. Besides, it is conceivable that were, let us say, some few hundred Eastern mothers-in-law of the uttermost-utmost type to descend on London with an eye to its conversion, as our unmarried Mission ladies do on India, full of sympathy born of their own needs, full of reprobation born of their own ideals, they would find quite as much at which to hold up holy hands of horror as we do—say in Calcutta and Bombay. What is more, were they to go into our country towns and villages, they would find far more at which to cavil than we can in rural India,

where life remains singularly pure, singularly
simple.

The intolerable indignity of a woman's position
generally, prey as she is to familiarities, to coarse
words in the streets, to gigglings and screechings
in corners, even to her husband's or lover's public
endearments, would shock them utterly. For
there is nothing of that sort in India. Vice
may thrive, but it is silent. Except in the bad-
character bazaars, and even there but seldom, there
is nothing to suggest sex in an Indian city. The
horse-play of hooligans, the open challenge of
Tam-o'-Shanter girls, the ticklings and titterings of
'Arry and 'Arriet, are alike unknown. There is
outward decency at least, and that is great gain.
Then the flaunting abroad of girls claiming attention by their dress, ready to rouse elemental
passions in all and sundry—if all and sundry are
foolish enough to be so roused,—while they smile,
securely amusing themselves, would be terrible.

That is not the woman's portion. If she spends
hours over her dress, it must be for the father
of her children, to attract him. The drunken
husbands, slatternly wives, miserably-neglected
children, would all be an offence indeed; while the
fact of a bride having often to work hard, instead

21

of being set free from care, would seem real cruelty. Last, but not least, the solitude of home life and the husband's incessant claim on his wife would be great hardships.

To us, on the other hand, it seems horrible to be screened, secluded, shut out from all outside pleasures, and we point out the pettinesses, the quarrelsomeness, which such idleness breeds in the Eastern women.

It is true, they are quarrelsome, they are petty, they are idle; indeed, idleness in the women of the towns—for in rural India the women do a lion's share of outdoor work—is responsible for much. I have known a large houseful of well-to-do native women do nothing at all from year's end to year's end, but talk, eat sweetmeats, and quarrel. Small wonder, then, if they spend their leisure in the formation of what their men-folk helplessly call "the woman's law"; that is a code of conduct, etiquette, ceremony, and observance, to comply with all the provisions of which would tax the resources of a Japanese general. To live as I have done in a Hindu house, especially when the real house-mistress is a masterful and deeply religious widow who is grandmother to the babies and mother to their parents, is no longer to wonder at

the absolute terror with which men speak of the *stri achchar.*

There is to be carrot stew for dinner, and the little cosmos licks its lips, until suddenly a child gets the hiccough, and straightway the fiat goes forth : carrot stew is unlucky, it must be pease porridge once more. The latest little bride perchance stumbles on the threshold, and hey presto ! such a to do. Red pepper must be burnt, soot smeared, and the whole household propitiate the little brass godlings on the roof with sweetmeats and flowers, lest evil befall high hopes. The wretched husbands in such houses, when they come home or go forth, have to submit to pattings, sprinklings, tying of knots in the hair, and are lucky if they have not to carry concealed about them to court, office, or workshop the most incongrous and sometimes revolting things, such as the half-chewed morsel of bread on which baby has cut his last tooth !

For the men of India are—poor souls !—the most henpecked in the world. They—especially the Mahommedans—make a brave show ; they may even, should they have some slight knowledge of English, stigmatise their women-folk as "poor ignorant idiots," but once behind the purdah in the

women's apartments, Bob Acres' courage is stable
in comparison with theirs. I know no more
pitiable object on this earth than an elderly Turk
having his beard dyed blue by his female relations !
Fatma and Ayesha wink at each other while the
other wives look on, and when the farce is over
they retire to the cupboard and lock themselves up
and give him the key, with strict injunctions to be
home punctually and not to look in at the club.
Of course, there are exceptions, but the general
form of Home Rule is feminine despotism veiled
by a slavish subserviency in trivial details.

Nothing, however, emphasises the different outlook of the Eastern and the Western women more
than the feelings with which, as a bride, the Eastern
and the Western girl goes to her husband's home.

The latter, no doubt, puts the husband first in
the list of agreeable novelties, but the new house,
the new position, the new liberty, run him very
close. She has herself chosen everything, the
cretonnes, the colour of the bridegroom's wedding
tie ; she has high hopes of her *cuisine*, of charming
dinners when she shall be admired as high priestess ;
and in these latter days there lurks deep down a
vague hope that motherhood may not come over-
soon to interfere with these pleasures.   Frankly, she

goes to the new life as she would go to the theatre, expecting to be interested and amused.

The Eastern bride goes to a restriction of liberty in a cloister; goes self-dedicate to duty. For her there is no new house, no new position, nothing but the extremely doubtful pleasure of a husband whom she has not chosen. No degradation could be deeper to her Western sister than being forced to marry a perfect paladin if she happened to prefer a pawnbroker; but the Indian woman is nine times out of ten quite content with the choice of others. There are indeed few happier households than Indian ones; or rather, one should perhaps use the past tense, since the native girl is fast learning to read novels, and ere long will doubtless grasp the fact that love makes the world go round—perhaps by turning people's heads!

It seems a pity; even the purdah is preferable to the titter of the Tam-o'-Shanter girl.

One thing is certain: the Western woman has quite as much to learn from the Eastern woman as the Eastern has from the Western. Were they both to set their minds to the task, they would come near to perfection. Meanwhile they—sisters of our Empire—eye each other, and, woman-like, complain of each other's manners.

Certainly one is free to confess that there are few more ill-mannered creatures on God's earth than a native lady travelling in a first- or second-class railway carriage, who considers her ticket entitles her to smoke, chew pan, suckle her baby, eat sweets, spit, and clean her teeth when and how she chooses.

But all women lose their manners when they are herded together, and so do men. Sex has its benefits.

Go to a Jat or a Sikh village where the women live in *bon camaraderie* with the men, and you will find yourself in a different atmosphere. Dip deeper down into the innermost thoughts of the women, and you will recognise that a good woman is a good woman all the world over.

And in India she is certainly none the less good, because behind all the senseless details, the almost revolting habits, and trivialities of real life, there lies an ideal of what woman should be, which is the highest that the world has ever known.

CHAPTER XV

No sketch of India would be complete without some mention of its ascetics, for they are the outward and visible sign of its inward and spiritual mind.

Long centuries of endless wars, conquests, famines, plagues, pestilence, have borne in upon this mind the vanity of earthly existence. All things are Maya or Illusion. The Secret of Life is how to escape from life.

The body is the first obstacle in the road; therefore let the body be got rid of by denying the desires of the body.

Here at once we get the *sadhu*, the man who has forsaken all things except that spark of the Divine which is himself. Naked, homeless, he eats only when food is offered to him, drinks only from the cup of cold water which is given in the name of the Lord.

In return he speaks to the givers, of the Great Secret and passes on, a wanderer.   In the days of Alexander the Great he was hoary of years; practically all Indian history has been enacted before his eyes.

"Naked he came, naked he has gone," is the death-wail of India.   The Sadhu anticipates it.

There are many kinds of ascetics in India, and they have many kinds of self-torture, but the true Sadhu is the one who simply forsakes all worldly things and wanders.

Smeared with ashes, their only dress (and that often out of fear of the police) a wisp of rag, they are generally dismissed by Anglo-Indians as ignorant, uncultured savages, or half-crazy fanatics.   But they are neither; they are often extremely well-educated, deeply versed in metaphysics and speculative lore, with a dialectic skill which is surprising. They will knock a false argument into a cocked hat with easy ability.   Some of them—these naked savages—will astonish you by quoting Herbert Spencer; for even nowadays they are recruited from all classes, and they belong by rights to the most thoughtful of each class.   In the West the thinker becomes an agnostic, or a parson, or a philanthropist; in India he becomes a Sadhu.

MID-DAY, JEYPORE

Naturally the majority of them—they may be roughly estimated at fifteen per cent of the total population—are not of very high mental calibre ; but, as a rule, these men whom you meet at every turn have all some kind of a hold on the spiritual life—they have all left something to follow nothing.

And they follow it far. Up in the mountain wilderness of Kashmir among the Eternal Snows, you may come upon a man who has journeyed on foot almost from Cape Cormorin, who has slept out under the stars, who has passed through the world, as it were, and carried nothing away with him, save the one Divine spark which he seeks to unite once more with the Great Mystery which lies behind all worlds. That man, count him how you will—let ignorance, superstition, even laziness and greed, be his chief motive powers—is yet a different being from the man who is absolutely occupied by this world. And many of these *yogis* are mighty thinkers. The fineness of their philosophical reasonings, the subtilty of their dialectics, leave one amazed.

I remember, on the way to the caves of Amar-nath, camping by chance (and mistake) on a plot of green sward which, it afterwards appeared, was a favourite resting-place of such ascetic pilgrims. They had no right to it, of course, but shortly after

22

our two small tents were up, a group of the naked
ones arrived, and began to grumble and cast sullen
looks at our Mahommedan servants.   They settled
down, however, for there was really plenty of room
for all, under their quaint mushroom-like white
umbrellas ; but as others kept dropping in until
there were a hundred or more of them, and the
murmuring grew to open cursing of the cook as he
returned with food from the gram-seller's shop, I
thought it time to interfere.   So, wrapping my
dress carefully round me, I started to walk
through their encampment affecting terror, and
calling out "Touch me not! touch me not!"
without the additional bad words which they had
used.

They stared, until one laughed.   And then we
were friends.   As other pilgrims drifted in I could
hear the word passed on, "She will not hurt, she is
a daughter of the Sun."   That evening there was a
regular symposium in the shade of a big banyan-tree,
and we talked politics for quite a long time very
amicably.   They left next morning, some of them
calling down blessings as they went.   I often
wonder if any of them succumbed to the snow-
drifts higher up, as countless numbers do, year after
year ; for they will take no precautions against the

cold, except perhaps a drink of "charrus" or Indian hemp.

Drug-drinking is a terrible temptation to these men, possibly, as Professor James remarks, because the effect of all intoxication is first of all to deaden the "spirit of fell denial" and bring communion with the Everlasting Yea. Certain it is that the drunkard begins nearly always by being a man of imagination; it is that, indeed, which makes drunkenness so great a curse, since it is *par excellence* the sin of the salt of the earth.

The Sadhu plays a heavy *rôle* in the daily life-history of India. He is generally the *guru* or godly teacher of every Indian household. To hear his call "*Alakh! Alakh!*" in the street is to rouse a pleasurable commotion in many a sheltered dovecot; for it is a pious duty to feed *sadhus,* and even the sternest house-mother will give a dole of cake and pease-pudding for that purpose.

Then they are still credited with miraculous powers, and many are the vows registered, as it were, in their name. Whether they have any occult knowledge or not, they certainly strive after it, especially those who pass their lives in self-torture and who hope thereby to gain a spiritual ascendancy over themselves and others. That the

people believe them to possess such power is
indubitable. A Yogi's curse is not a thing to be
put aside lightly.   Indeed, there are too many
curious coincidences following an interference with
their rights and privileges, even amongst Europeans,
not to make wonder grow as to whether some of
them, at any rate, are not passed masters in what
we Westerns have begun to dabble in—hypnotism.
That nearly all the so-called occultism of India is
due to this possibility of getting hold of the minds
of others, and making them see what you wish
them to see, hear what you wish them to hear, is
extremely likely; for the native is peculiarly
prone, by reason of his emotional, mystical, and
imaginative temperament, to follow any mental
lead-over.   He is, in fact, impressionable to an
exaggerated degree.

In Indian folk-lore the Yogi is the Giver of Gifts,
the fairy godmother, and even in everyday life he
is believed to have many beneficent arts. He has
the power of bestowing children, of turning the
baser metals to gold, of bringing good or bad luck.
Naturally these yielded pretensions are the parents
of much fraud and deception. Half the idle tales
of India are concerned with disreputable *yogis* of
sorts who generally manage to get themselves out

of deserved scrapes by the quickness of their wits.
But these very stories, taken in conjunction with
the persistent belief in some occult power obtain-
able by prayer, fasting, meditation, tend to show
that such a conviction has some firm basis on which
to rest.   Otherwise, long ere this the belief would
be confined to the ignorant.   But it is not.
Educated natives are often loth to speak of such
things, but deep down in their hearts they have
no doubt that by practising *yoga* all things are
possible.

These wanderers, then, begging their way from
house to house — often not even begging, but
pausing at a reverential call to take a handful of
parched corn, a drink of water,—are the outward
and visible signs of India's inward and spiritual
grace, the grace of vivid realisation of the Higher
World in which all things live, and move, and
have their being.

It is difficult even to imagine what may be
termed the *sadhu* system applied to the West; to
think of John Jones, Stockbroker, suddenly struck
by the mutability, the instability of shares, getting
up one morning and saying good-bye for ever to
his portly wife. his many children, slipping off his
decent go-to-city suit, and, without a penny in his

pocket, starting to walk from Mincing Lane to John o' Groat's House, and so round by the Giant's Causeway and the Land's End. He would be in an asylum before the first week was out.

But in India this happens every day. Out of one family and another, some one possessed by a hunger after righteousness drifts away, and his place knows him no more.

In his stead there is one more wanderer, one more ash-smeared figure which may appear suddenly in the shade of a village mango tope, silent, immovable, inscrutable. The years may pass on, and still he may sit there eating so little that by and by the legend grows up that he eats not at all, and the people from the neighbouring villages come and worship the Mystery of all Things behind the visible mystery. Then one day the place knows him no more. He is not there. He has vanished whence he came, and whether he is dead or whether he has wandered on, none know.

CHAPTER XVI

THE MORALS OF INDIA

MEGASTHENES, who lived in India three hundred years before Christ, records, through the pen of Arrian, his impressions of the Hindu race.

"They are remarkably brave. They are also remarkable for simplicity and integrity ; so reasonable as never to have recourse to a law-suit ; so honest as neither to require locks to their doors nor writings to bind their agreements. No Indian was ever known to tell an untruth."

Now this is an account at which most Anglo-Indians would laugh scornfully, or exclaim, "How are the mighty fallen !" for the impression that our Aryan brother is far beyond us in deceit, untruthfulness, and general untrustworthiness is very strong. In such matters, however, one can but appeal to one's own personal experiences, and my own bear out the assertion that truth lies at the bottom of a well. It certainly has no home in East or West; but one suffers more from this fact in the latter, because telling a lie is there looked upon in a much more serious light. In India the utterer is not by any means bound to support the lie; he can take it back and make it over again without much loss in personal dignity. Discovered in an untruth, he can hold his ears with both hands, say "*tobah*" (I repent), and there the incident ends. In the West, once a lie, always a lie, which must be upheld at all costs, even to the making of more lies.

Absolutely false and quite irresponsible witness on oath is undoubtedly more common in India than it is in England; but there is equally no doubt whatever that Abstract Truth as seldom finds its way into an English Court of Justice as it does into an Indian one. The amount of disingenuous bias and almost wilful failure to see things as they really are, is greater with the more complex mind. The Indian lie, briefly, is more conscious; the English one is glossed over by inaccuracies, wilful blinding of the eyes, wilful cooking of the mental accounts.

Then in regard to the adulteration of food and general untrustworthiness in commerce, there can be no question as to where heinousness of offence lies. It is rapidly becoming impossible to rely on the word of any tradesman in England, while the only way to secure food that you have chosen and bought is to take it away with you. A recent discussion in a daily paper has produced the assertion that without some measure of fraud it would be impossible in England for a small trader to live by his trade. India can scarcely go "one better" than this. In fact, the only point on which to advance on that one is to substitute for our proverb which bids us believe but one half of what we hear, the advice to believe but one half of what we see and nothing of what we hear.

All this may fail to convince many that the native of India is not a more inveterate liar than is his European brother; but if they consider how comparatively easy it is to find out a lie when but little stigma attaches to the telling of it, and also how comparatively difficult it is to the more simple mind to evade the more complex one, the conclusion may be reached that all over the world Truth runs a poor chance in the mouth of many men. Whole races, like that of the Welsh and the Maltese, are given over to an absolute incapacity for telling it, so that insistent asseveration of a

thing having or not having occurred is the strongest
ground for believing the contrary to be the case,
and a mistress, when her maid, on being asked for
something, replies, "May God strike me dead if I
ever see it," can say with confidence—and the best
results—"Go and fetch it at once."

There is another blame thrown wrongfully, so
far as my personal experience goes, on the native
of India : that is ingratitude. It is even asserted
that so marked is the absence of the positive
virtue that no term exists in the vernacular ex-
pressive of "thank you."

This is hardly accurate. No one who has lived
with Mahommedans can have failed to hear the
word *Shukr* used exactly as our recognition is
used for any action that requires specific thanks,
while the cheerful "Good" which one hears so
often everywhere holds in it a hint of all-round
praise not far from personal gratitude.

Under any circumstances the ignoring of a claim
to thanks for the performing of small kindnesses
may conceivably be due to other things than a lack
of gratitude !

In regard to actual gratitude for favours
received, one must admit that in India, as elsewhere, it is apt to be alloyed by the hope of

A NARROW STREET

1

favours to come. On the other hand, such gratitude is very real, very absorbing. Nothing delights the soul of a native more than to have a patron. He begins hero-worshipping early by giving himself heart and soul to his *guru* or teacher. It is part of his creed. So, when in after life he finds any one whom he can call his father and mother, he does so promptly, and with appalling simplicity flings himself and his family on their care.

"But you are my patron—my father and mother," is often a pained reproach when some quite impossible favour is refused.

There is, however, one absolute refutation of this charge of ingratitude against the native of India, and that is the penny post! Every mail-day brings to England, to Englishmen on leave, or even to those who have retired from the services, a perfect cataract of letters. Indeed, the persistency with which the native will write to his patron is quite pathetic; so is the number of persons to whom he will confidently look up as his father and mother. Twenty, five and twenty years of absence is no bar to his remembrance of them, and long after the memories of Bishan Das, Moolchund, Afzool Khan, and half-a-dozen other clerks, contractors, and chuprassies have become inextricably mixed up in the mind of some retired Anglo-Indian, mail-day will lay on his breakfast-table letters which will set him thinking "Where was it that I knew that fellow ?"

In regard to theft, of which the native is universally accused by his Anglo-Indian masters. In this, again, an appeal to personal experience would bring forward one solitary case of theft in the East as against innumerable cases in the West. Each person must judge by their own experience; but mine is, emphatically, that for pure pilfering the native servant is not in it with English servants. Possibly it is only the restriction of caste and creed which keeps the fingers of the former off the larder, but if any one wants to test the relative position let him put out some chocolate creams as if for dessert and note the results !

Of course, for absolutely unutterable dishonesty there is no race in the world like the Latin race. And they have no respect of persons. Now in India one thing is certain: the native seldom steals from his own master. But then a master is to him a personality. He is not a mere employer, who, like a corporation, has neither a soul to be damned nor a body to be kicked. There is still in India the old-fashioned virtue of faithfulness to the salt you eat; a virtue that has long since become unfashionable in England.

Another accusation against the native is that he is detestably litigious. This is true. And he becomes more so day by day. But this is a growth of later years, and it is instructive to consider how it came about. To begin with, doubtless, there were high hopes of justice. The idea of a fair field and no favour brought endless disputes into our courts. These hopes were fulfilled in a percentage of cases. The odds between the old-fashioned bribery of the lower officials and the new inaccessibility of the higher were sufficiently even to make a lottery out of a law-suit. There was, there could be, no foregone conclusion. So a game ensued in which the devil would take the hindmost in skill. To the majority of litigants in India a law-suit is a form of sport, and it is high time that the court fees should be raised. The most serious aspect of our legal administration is the ease with which false criminal charges can be trumped up. Given a single friend in the police, and your enemy is at your mercy absolutely.

Murder bulks largely in the criminal statistics, doubtless because of the disregard of death which the religion of India brings with it. As a unit, the native is not afraid of death, and he will deal it out with comparative calm to others. The institution of Thuggi, now happily repressed, is a case in point. Here men vowed themselves to a religion of murder, and made an often precarious livelihood by it, their death-dealing serving the double purpose of satisfying their stomachs and the Great Death-mother's claims on all men. It was a curious cult with its casting of lots before the Lord for the exact day, hour, and place in which the deed was to be done.

To pass on to what is generally hinted at when the word morality is used. There can be no question that in the villages all over India sexual morality stands excessively high. Even our missionaries admit that compared with the conduct of our rural and working classes the standard is good. My own experience is that it is very good. The very measure of infinite disgrace which attaches to infidelity and illegitimacy is proof positive of this. In all my years of life in India I never came across but one girl, amongst all the thousands of girls who passed through my

hands, who had, as the phrase runs, "got into trouble," and she literally wept herself to death over the shame of it. Here grandmothers accept the charge of their illegitimate grandchildren willingly, because they are paid half-a-crown a week for their keep.

It is well to tell the truth solidly sometimes, and the truth is this: in sexual matters, despite the hoary old wickedness of Indian towns, their almost inconceivable viciousness, and the open claims of the courtezan class, the standard of national morality is far higher in India than it is in England.

Then they are inconceivably kind to children. The ill-usage, at any rate to the beating point, of wives, is rare, while their affection and care for their parents sets an example to every Christian country in the world. There is in India no squeezing of a son by the Poor Law to produce a miserable shilling a week for the support of an aged and widowed mother, and the father to extreme old age is still the honoured patriarch. We Westerns need to consider all these good points ere we reach out our hands to the mote in our brother's eye.

There are plenty of motes, Heaven knows; but the West has its beam.

CHAPTER XVII

"1857"

THE date has an ugly sound to English ears, and yet it marks our flood level in India. Never before had we touched, never again shall we touch, that height of heroism which once and for all branded India as part of the Empire.

We had held it till then as a commercial speculation. Glossed over by much philanthropical policy, the ultimate sixpence still sat enthroned as the real ruler of India, if only because it was the lineal descendant of the "mutual and friendly trafique" of Queen Elizabeth's first famous letter to Akbar; in which, by the way, she comments on the "singular report that is of your Imperial Majestie's humanitie in these uttermost parts of the world."

In fact, if we are to understand the position which led up to the great Mutiny, we must face the truth, namely, that for two hundred and fifty years our tenure of India had had a monetary basis, although certainly for the last fifty of those years we had done our level best to combine business with justice.

Curiously enough, it was this awakening of the national conscience in regard to India which led to the terrors of '57.

In the old days we had taken our money, justly or unjustly, and gone on our way. Now we stayed to criticise, to inquire, to amend and alter the way in which that money had been made.

A princeling, if devoid of money for tribute, would have a Resident sent to his court to spy out his actions if he was suspected of laying wholesale hands on his subjects' savings; yet the money had to be forthcoming all the same. Reading the history of the English in India, it is impossible not to admit that their eyes were ever open to the main chance and that the trend of their mind was towards annexation; the mere fact that by 1857 we had absorbed almost the whole of India proves that this was so. That many, nay, most of its rulers were utterly unworthy, dissolute to a degree, does not alter the evidence which shows that we took advantage of every point we could to get a

24

grip on the land.   The right of adoption admitted
by Hindu and Mahommedan law—a very lenient
law it must be confessed, leaving no less than three
years to a disconsolate widow in which to bring
forward an heir to her dead husband—stood in our
way many a time, and so adoption had to be, not a
right, but a special privilege.   This was a blow at
the whole status of these petty chiefs.   Childless-
ness was no uncommon result of their depraved
habits, and this right of adoption had been, so to
speak, the safeguard of the libertine.   Now the
Company stepped in, appropriating the fiefs.

In 1852 Sattara was so annexed.   In 1853 the
case of the Rajaship of Kerauli was the cause of
much heartburning, and though that was finally
decided in favour of the adopted heir, it left its
mark in the bitter controversy which the very next
year arose concerning Jhansi.   Here once more
the argument that the Company, though bound
by treaty to uphold "heirs and successors," was
not bound to consider the claims of a successor
other than a lineal descendant, prevailed against
the widow's assertion that the Persian word
employed included not only heirs of the body
but of the mind—that is to say, "any one whom
the chief adopted as his son to perform those

funeral rites which are necessary to insure beatitude."

Jhansi therefore shared the fate of Sattara, to be followed in the very same year by the annexation of Nagpur. Concerning this, the view of one member of Council innocently lets the cat out of the bag. "Believing in the dispensation of Providence," he writes, "I cannot coincide in any view of this matter which shall have for its object the maintenance of native rule against the progress of events which throws undisputed power into our possession."

No more is needed. "God is on our side, let His enemies be scattered." Against that conviction naught avails; not even truth. And this belief, almost fanatical in its yearning to "gather the heathen into the fold," had come to India with the wave of Evangelicalism which about this time literally swept the services. And so we find the names of many truly Christian heroes as participators in the greatest act of injustice that was ever perpetrated in India, the annexation of Oude on the 6th May 1856—just one year before the outbreak at Meerut on the 10th May 1857. The facts are too clear for any doubt whatever. In 1887 we entered into a distinct treaty with the

Nawabs of Oude in which certain penalties were set forth in the event of bad government. Annexation was not one of them.

In '57, nearly twenty years after, we politely tendered to the Nawab our regret at having failed to inform him that this treaty had never been ratified by the Directors, though it had been by mistake "included in a volume of treaties which was published in 1845 by the authority of Government." We admitted this to be "embarrassing"; not sufficiently so, however, to prevent "action."

No notice was awarded to the fact that if the treaty of 1837 was null and void, the previous one of 1801 stood unabrogated. By this we could either force the Nawab to comply with our demands for better government, or withdraw our guarantee for support, giving back the territories ceded in exchange to us for this guarantee of military aid.

This did not suit our policy. We therefore, without one shadow of excuse, annexed Oude.

This same wave of Evangelicalism had brought about other dangers. Our officials, after acquiescing in Indian manners in the past, had begun to busy themselves over the moral welfare of those entrusted to their charge. Missionaries were

coming out in shoals, girls' schools being started,
zenana classes thought of, and, naturally, with the
advent of English ladies a great outcry was raised
regarding the position of women.   Suttee had
already been made illegal, and though the Emperor
Akbar had issued precisely the same order without
raising any dissatisfaction, our methods were not
so successful.   The last straw was the passing
of the Widows' Remarriage Act; an absolutely
inoffensive Act in itself.

But the times were bad.   And yet when revolt
did come, it was a purely military revolt—one
which might, which should have been crushed.
The least forethought, the least understanding,
the least just, stern consideration would have
averted it.

To grasp the truth of this, let us imagine a man
like John Nicholson at the head of every native
regiment.   Where would the chance of mutiny
have been then?

There is nothing in the wide world more
sickening than to read the minutes of evidence in
the Barrackpore courts-martial.   Many of the
English officers were evidently unable to speak the
language of their subordinates.

But it came—came suddenly, almost unexpectedly; and assuredly none who read the plain, unvarnished tale of that fatal parade at Meerut can wonder that it did come.

And then—then it is a story for tears, a story of utter incompetence.

For there was really no plot, really no settled collusion between Meerut and Delhi. The long six weeks of the King's trial, during which no stone was left unturned to implicate him if possible, prove this beyond measure of doubt.

But, as I have written elsewhere, "Englishmen live to make mistakes and die to retrieve them." So the incompetence was paid for; ay, and more than that—even the ultimate sixpence was blotted out of the record, East *versus* West, by the river of blood which flowed for close on two years.

It was that fateful pause of close on a month before the first blow was returned which, for a time at least, turned the purely military mutiny into an organised revolt; though, even then, the mass of India went about its patient, humdrum life, heedless, even ignorant, of what was happening, it might be but a few miles off.

"Did you see anything of the 'Great Evil Days'?" I asked an old woman once.

"Huzoor, yes!" was the reply. "We women

were sitting spinning at the door one day when a band of riders appeared. We screamed; but they only took everything to eat that we had in the house, and then galloped on their ways. We wondered who they were. The grandmother said they were Toorks, for sure—they used to come in the old days. But afterwards we heard that wicked men had rebelled. Hai hai!"

That was all which thousands, ay, millions, of the people of India knew of the storm which shook England to its foundations—to its very foundations. For only those who went through it can have any idea of the flood-tide of passionate sorrow, and indignation, and hate, and desire for revenge, which swept through the land from one end to the other.

There is no sadder reading in the world than the daily papers of June, July, August, and September 1857, especially the Anglo-Indian papers. Even clergymen rushed into print, denouncing the Laodicean Government, pointing to the massacres as God's punishment for trafficking with the Devil, and calling on the nation to smite and spare not.

And it smote; how deep it is perhaps wiser not to say, for it was unavoidable. Only the clear-sighted and strong-minded kept their heads, with the cry of women and little children in their ears ; and these clear-sighted, strong-minded ones were those who, overtopping their comrades, fell the first beneath Death's levelling scythe, leaving the less masterful minds to take the lead when the time for revenge had come.

Regarding the outbreak itself, it is extremely difficult to give anything like a consecutive history. Delhi, Agra, Lucknow, Cawnpore, and, later on, Jhansi, were all centres round which a series of coeval and yet totally distinct incidents gathered.

Delhi gains in significance, because here we faced our foe as the assailant.   Here we struggled, not desperately for dear life, but for conquest. That is what gives the Red Ridge at Delhi its distinction.   There we were really fighting—though for a while we did not seem to realise it—not as a lioness defending her cubs, but as a lion waiting for its spring of revenge.

I have often wondered, indeed, if the one woman who, thrusting herself upon the Ridge, remained there with indomitable courage through thick and thin, ever realised how that perfectly useless courage spoilt what should have been the red rock's inviolable manhood ; but then one grows hypercritical in dreaming over what will surely go

down to the last limit of time as the highest flood-mark of the Anglo-Saxon race.

To return to history. Beginning, as all know, on Sunday the 10th May, the outbreak had a month of inaction in which to spread. It was the 7th of June ere a single retaliatory blow was struck; and even after that we hesitated and vacillated for two long months, until John Nicholson appeared, and straightway began the attack.

On the 14th of September he took Delhi, losing his life needlessly, uselessly, in himself trying to rally a regiment that was spent past repair. It is sad to walk in the full blaze of the Indian sun down the narrow lane leading to the Burn Bastion and measure the distance which must have lain—full of that blaze of yellow sunshine—between the man who cried, "It can be done," and those whose every fibre gave out the note, "It cannot." Saddest of all to realise that, whether we see it or not, there is always an aureole of empty sunlight between men like John Nicholson and their fellows. He died on the day after the Palace was occupied, the King taken prisoner, and the Princes shot. Regarding the latter incident, let each decide for himself if Hodson was right or wrong in what he did. But two things seem fairly certain:

Hodson's orders regarding any promise of safety were stringent, and there was no attempt at swift rescue.

There stands on the Ridge now a terribly Gothic (not to say Vandalistic) Memorial to that third of the total force of Englishmen who fell before Delhi. But an edict cut on the red rocks would have been more to the purpose. One can dream how it might have run, modelled on the lines of Asoka the Loving-minded One's rock-inscribed decrees :—

I, the Beloved of my People, Victoria, do hereby declare peace on earth and goodwill towards all men.

It would have been better than strings of un-meaning names,—names that even in life only represented units of an attacking force. But we need to learn from the Japanese how to die, not as units, but as one great whole.

For the rest, in almost every large station in India there are relics in story or site of some heroism on the part of the Masters.

It is well that this should be so ; well also that neither the white face nor the dark one should forget the struggle of '57. But there is one thing which the white face needs to remember.

If ever a race brought revolt on itself, we did so in India. Therefore we should remember with gladness that for every native who even inactively sided against us, there were a hundred who remained loyal.

CHAPTER XVIII

THE ANGLO-INDIAN

ENGLAND does not half appreciate the full value of her Anglo-Indian sons. Authors have sung their vices rather than their virtues, and the steady doggedness with which a man, bereaved of wife and children, a prey to discomfort and dejection, will plod through the weary work of a long hot-weather day remains still without its due crown of laurel.

Yet nothing is finer; nothing in the whole history of the world is more worthy praise.

One has to read the impressions of foreign visitors to India before grasping this. Scarcely one of them has not spent a page or two in un-stinted admiration of the ordinary Anglo-Indian official. In truth, his patient endurance of much evil is marvellous; for it is only given to the few to feel India anything but an exile.

To most men fresh from the universities, brimful of culture, instinct with desire to live, the dull round of Indian duty, the impossibility of any real intercourse with the natives, and the prohibition which the climate, for a large portion of the year, puts upon games and sports, must all be dreary indeed.

And yet behind all the dreariness lies the glamour. Most of them feel it, if not during the time of their service, at least when that service is over. Then India, giving up the body, claims the soul.

One of the most curious points about the work which the Anglo-Indian does is the absolute ignorance concerning it which exists in England. Here we have a community which for generations on generations has sent sons and daughters to this dependency of the Crown; which has not sent them out once and for all as it might have done to Canada or Australia, but which has received them and their children back again to its very heart, full as they must be of strange new life, and which has not in any way grasped what that life is or realised its procedure.

Even most Englishwomen know partially how England is governed, but few Englishmen who have not been in India have the faintest idea of how we rule it. The curse of forgetfulness seems on them. You tell them, you elaborately explain the system, and the next time you meet, lo! they have forgotten entirely, or at most remember that Lord Macaulay, in addition to writing a History of England, compiled India's Penal Code. A fine compilation too, in its broad concurrent lines of law and justice.

This curious inability to assimilate India is still more striking when we deal with Englishwomen, who often return from a lifetime spent there absolutely untouched by its influence. This is a far more common state of affairs than it used to be. Possibly the closer touch with the home country which has been brought about by improved communications may have something to do with this. On the other hand, signs are not wanting that the patience of English men and women will not long outlast the many privileges which in the old time made exile endurable. The value of money has decreased enormously, yet pay remains the same; the power which was more to many a man than gold has been largely curtailed. To feel that you have the welfare of thousands in your grip, and to know yourself a mere machine, paid inadequately to grind out so-called justice to suit the hair-splitting of "bannisters" fresh from the pettinesses of English procedure, are two very different postulates. Small wonder is it that in India itself the gulf between the rulers and the ruled is widening. There is a half-hidden race hatred nowadays which did not exist fifty years ago,—no! not even when the shambles of the Mutiny were fresh in men's minds.

Then, both the white and the dark faces forgave. Now they pass each other by with a challenge on one side, the cut direct on the other.

For this education is largely responsible. In the hands of scientific experts it is fast becoming the curse of humanity. To them a scholar is a scholar whether he be Esquimaux or Hottentot, and must be turned out to pattern at all costs, regardless of the uses to which he will subsequently be put; and—what is even more disastrous—quite regardless of the germ-plasm which lies at the back of all education.

So, not until many many generations of slowly acquired mental and physical deviation from the type have come to obliterate much that lies at the back of the Eastern brain, can we hope to educate it on Western lines to a Western ideal. The

attempt to turn the two hemispheres out to one
pattern by superficial education is like attempting
to dye cotton and wool in the same vat. The
sooner we learn this the better.

In the meantime, rightly or wrongly, there is
every day growing up amongst Anglo-Indians the
feeling that in any dispute with a native they will,
for political reasons, be put to the wall. It does
not tend to soften manners or promote fellowship,
and its existence is a sign of ineptitude on the part
of authority. For the English, taking them as a
whole, are a just race, and to rouse a general sense
of injustice in them needs injustice.

Yet even so curtailed, as they doubtless are,
of power and position, there is still to be found,
generally in remote districts, some Anglo-Indian
who is literally a father to the people under him;
who in cholera or plague time will issue absolutely
illegal orders for their benefit, which are as absolutely
obeyed; who drives a coach and four through silly
High Court circulars; who lives beloved, and dies
to be canonised,—unless, indeed, to some such
man, capable, full of common sense, instinct with
a desire for duty, there comes some hair-splitting
stickler for rules and regulations, and in the ensuing
quarrel the best man goes down disgraced.

A VEGETABLE MARKET, PESHAWUR

Such things have happened, are happening, and the result is naturally to exalt the commonplace. Even in his free day John Nicholson lived in conflict with the authorities; but three months ere he took Delhi and saved India he had begged to be transferred from the Punjab while he could still go with honour.

John Nicholsons are a product of the past. They would be an impossibility to-day; and yet India would be none the worse for them. Nothing is more striking than the way in which any excess of vitality above the normal impresses the native. It does not matter in what way the vitality is displayed, whether in work or play, mind or body, the native follows on instinctively. And if to the vitality we add imagination, the result is such legendary hero-worship as that accorded to the Emperor Akbar and to many an Englishman besides John Nicholson.

Taking him all in all, the Anglo-Indian is a product of which the Empire may well be proud. It is no small task for an alien race to govern close on three hundred millions of people dispersed through close on two millions of square miles, especially when, in the process of government, no less than one hundred and forty-seven different

26

dialects have to be considered,—more especially when we grasp the amazing fact that there are under one hundred and fifty thousand of that alien race all told, or one to every two thousand natives of India.

That the government is expensive goes without saying. The question remains whether a cheaper one would be as effective, or whether the cheapness would simply be on paper, and the pockets of the people suffer privately instead of publicly. Certain it is that in almost every part of India the cry is still "Send not my case to the court of a black judge." It is an unfair cry, since there can be no question as to the increase of probity in the newer race of native officials; but it will be a long, long time before bribery and corruption is swept away from an Indian court, white or black. At present the distinction between them is purely one of degree; that is to say, how high the scale of bribery can rise. It is to be doubted whether any case in India was ever decided without some money—even if it only be eight annas—changing hands, below board. If not in the court itself, then in the police office; for a purging of the police force from its present abuses is one of the most pressing problems in India. How to give it sufficient power and at the same time limit its possibilities of oppression has hitherto been an insoluble puzzle. Higher pay may do something. At present it is idle to ask, as we ask, an educated man to wield authority and keep his hands free of palm oil, on a salary at which a household drudge would grumble.

So much for the Anglo-Indian,—a hard-worked man, whether he be judge or tax-collector, canal officer, doctor, policeman or soldier.

There remains his wife, of whom so much has been written and might still be written. Of this, however, there seems to be no manner of doubt: it is between the women of England and the women of India that the solution of the problem "How to rule and be ruled" lies. The one great unalterable split between East and West is in their relative Ideals of Perfect Womanhood. Let, then, the sister subjects take heed to their ways; let them remember that all give and no take is quite as demoralising to both parties as the converse. I do not think that we women have yet made up our hands decisively for the Great Game of Life. There is time yet for cards to be cast away and fresh ones taken in.

We in the West are talking of discarding

marriage; but, played in Eastern fashion, marriage
has guarded much that woman holds most dear.

So if nothing else is yielded to that Eastern
fashion, it may at least be granted a cool and
courteous consideration.

CHAPTER XIX

THE PROBLEM OF INDIA

INDIA is full of problems, the first and greatest of all being to the Englishman how to get through each successive hot weather; for hidden away in this mere question of personal discomfort lies a very large question.

How long can we—a race who, owing to the climate, cannot bring up our children in India—remain lords paramount of the soil; for *we* are the Government, and the Government is absolute owner of every inch of land? It is true that what with permanently assessed land-tax here, and the rights of hereditary tenants there, we have frittered away much of our sovereign power uselessly, idly; but the land from time immemorial was the Crown's, and only the Crown's.

But it is evident we cannot colonise it. Nature has decreed that we remain in India on sufferance.

Are we to remain so always, spending our best years, giving our best lives to India, or are we by and by to take off our hats and say politely, "That is enough, you can fend for yourselves"?

That is a great problem ; and the second is like unto it. In what condition ought we in this case to leave India? Shall she be attired in the latest Paris fashion, or should she be dressed in a manner more suitable to the climate?

So far the answer has been unhesitatingly "the Paris frock." For the last fifty years we have done our best by every means in our power to "raise" the standard of personal comfort in India. To a certain extent we have succeeded. It is not nearly so easy for the very poor to live as it used to be. There is a greater variation between their status and the status of the rich. In the old days, from one end to the other of India, the people, rich or poor, lived mostly on the food staple of their particular country—wheat where it was wheat, rice where it was rice. A little more clarified butter and sugar for the rich, a little less for the poor —therein lay the chief difference between them. They were housed in much the same fashion. The palace was larger than the hovel, more decorated, but both alike were devoid of luxury. Even now

A BULLOCK-CART, AJMERE

in conservative palaces there is no furniture, — a table, a chair or two for the convenience of Europeans or Europeanised natives; for the rest, often tattered carpets and string beds. Some years ago when the chief of perhaps the richest State in India lay sick of typhoid fever, the English doctor asked for a teaspoon. There was not one. Salt, sugar, everything was laid before His Highness in a leaf, and he helped himself with his fingers.

Only the other day some philanthropical ladies were shocked at their horrified complaints that the poor plague patients actually had no sheets to their beds being met by a hearty laugh. There are no sheets or towels in India.

Fine clothes, rich jewels, and a redundancy of fat differentiated the Raja from his ryots ; little else.

Are we to change this simplicity of life if we can, by our shibboleth of raising the standard of personal comfort? Are we to preach our Gospel of Ease for the few, and inoculate India with all its resulting discomfort for the many? There is no poor law in India : none is necessary. The patriarchal system and religious charity supply its place.

Are we to discourage this, levy a poors' rate, and build workhouses? Is it necessary for the due mental progress of India that her sons should be educated to admire the *Spectator*, and translate Tennyson's "Lotos-Eaters" into Urdu doggrel?

Not long ago all these minor evils were considered to be inevitably bound up in all true progress. Pauperism was its lineal descendant. Some one must be left behind in the race. The conflict of classes, the over specialisation of the individual both in work and play, the Trades-Union doctrine of labour limited by the lowest and not by the highest,—these, and many another palpably immoral position had to be borne with for the sake of civilisation.

But of late a people have sprung forth to take their first place among the nations who give the lie to these shibboleths. The Japanese are showing the world how to reap all the benefits of culture, of art, and commerce, and science, without gathering in also the tares which have grown up with the wheat in the West.

They have astonished that Western world by their curious, unhesitating collectivism. To them Japan seems no aggregation of separate interests, of clashing, conflicting desires. They seem to have grasped the unity of mind which lies behind the multiplicity of matter, and they carry the simplicity which is born of this belief into their everyday life.

But if they have astonished the West, if they have even roused in it vague doubts as to whether its boasted civilisation has not grown up on false lines, what have they done for those Eastern nations who now, for the first time in history, see the victory lie in the great battle for precedence with *their* thoughts, *their* philosophies?

In regard to India, at any rate, it is not too much to say that the one topic of the bazaar is Japan. Its successes are magnified a thousand-fold, its possible future foretold with all the imagination of a fairy tale.

That this enthusiastic approval has one good result is evident: in all probability India would rise as one man were Japan's enemy to invade it. On the other hand, such an example must rouse restlessness, and lead to questionings as to whether it is indeed necessary to swallow our civilisation whole-sale, pauper asylums, divorce courts, foundling hospitals, Stock Exchange, and all.

If it would only cause such questionings amongst the rulers as well as the ruled, some of the many problems of India would be solved.

And of what a dustpanful of sheer rubbish should we not rid ourselves!

We should then have a distinct policy instead of,

as now, one that shifts and changes with every change of party government.

Take one problem only, the problem of our Indian army. We have organised it, and organised it well, on purely Western lines, but we have not taken into account the curious Eastern view of soldiering which of old made the presence of a legal wife and family almost a disgrace in cantonments.

These remained at home, and, as there was practically no standing army in our sense of the word, their husbands could return to them every few years.

Now, without reverting to this, we could easily achieve the same result by enlisting double the number of men, and allowing one-half of them to be at home on, say, two years' leave. When they returned to the colours those who had served for two years would return to their farms.

But there are so many similar difficulties which might be smoothed over, if only the rulers did not consider it their duty to use Western salves.

Meanwhile India goes on in her tutelage, and goes on well.

The question is, Might she not go one better?

INDEX

211

Printed by R. & R. CLARK, LIMITED, *Edinburgh*.

IN THE SAME SERIES

ALL WITH PAGE ILLUSTRATIONS IN COLOUR

EACH 20s. NET

"Of all God's gifts to the sight of man, colour is the holiest, the most Divine, the most solemn."—*Ruskin*.

"All men completely organized and justly tempered enjoy colour; it is meant for the perpetual comfort and delight of the human heart."—*Ruskin*.

DESCRIBED BY SIR MARTIN CONWAY
PAINTED BY A. D. M'CORMICK

THE ALPS

70 FULL-PAGE ILLUSTRATIONS IN COLOUR

TEXT BY MARCUS B. HUISH, LL.B.

BRITISH WATER-COLOUR ART, ETC.

60 OF THE KING'S PICTURES IN COLOUR

PAINTED BY MORTIMER MENPES, R.I., R.E.
DESCRIBED BY DOROTHY MENPES

BRITTANY

75 FULL-PAGE ILLUSTRATIONS IN COLOUR

PAINTED AND DESCRIBED BY
R. TALBOT KELLY, R.B.A.

BURMA

75 FULL-PAGE ILLUSTRATIONS IN COLOUR

PAINTED BY HENRY B. WIMBUSH
DESCRIBED BY EDITH F. CAREY

THE CHANNEL ISLANDS

76 FULL-PAGE ILLUSTRATIONS IN COLOUR

TEXT BY JOSEPH GREGO

CRUIKSHANK'S WATER-COLOURS

68 FULL-PAGE FACSIMILE REPRODUCTIONS IN COLOUR

BY MORTIMER MENPES, R.I.
TEXT BY DOROTHY MENPES

THE DURBAR

100 FULL-PAGE ILLUSTRATIONS IN COLOUR

PAINTED AND DESCRIBED BY R. TALBOT KELLY, R.B.A.

EGYPT

75 FULL-PAGE ILLUSTRATIONS IN COLOUR

BY HELEN ALLINGHAM, R.W.S.
TEXT BY MARCUS B. HUISH

HAPPY ENGLAND

80 FULL-PAGE ILLUSTRATIONS IN COLOUR

PAINTED BY A. HEATON COOPER
DESCRIBED BY WILLIAM PALMER

THE ENGLISH LAKES

75 FULL-PAGE ILLUSTRATIONS IN COLOUR

PAINTED BY COL. R. C. GOFF
DESCRIBED BY MRS. GOFF

FLORENCE AND SOME TUSCAN CITIES

75 FULL-PAGE ILLUSTRATIONS IN COLOUR

BY M. H. SPIELMANN, F.S.A.,
AND G. S. LAYARD

KATE GREENAWAY

75 FULL-PAGE ILLUSTRATIONS (51 IN COLOUR) AND NUMEROUS ILLUSTRATIONS IN THE TEXT

BY NICO JUNGMAN
TEXT BY BEATRIX JUNGMAN

HOLLAND

76 FULL-PAGE ILLUSTRATIONS IN COLOUR

PAINTED BY JOHN FULLEYLOVE, R.I.
DESCRIBED BY THE REV. JOHN KELMAN, M.A.

THE HOLY LAND

92 FULL-PAGE ILLUSTRATIONS, MOSTLY IN COLOUR

BY MORTIMER MENPES, R.I.
TEXT BY FLORA A. STEEL

INDIA

75 FULL-PAGE ILLUSTRATIONS IN COLOUR

PAINTED BY FRANCIS S. WALKER, R.H.A.
DESCRIBED BY FRANK MATHEW

IRELAND

77 FULL-PAGE ILLUSTRATIONS IN COLOUR

PUBLISHED BY A. & C. BLACK, SOHO SQUARE, LONDON, W.

IN THE SAME SERIES

ALL WITH PAGE ILLUSTRATIONS IN COLOUR

ILLUSTRATED IN THE SAME STYLE
AS THE 20s. SERIES

PRICE 7s. 6d. NET EACH

PAINTED BY WM. SMITH, JUN.
DESCRIBED BY THE REV. W. S. CROCKETT
ABBOTSFORD
20 FULL-PAGE ILLUSTRATIONS IN COLOUR

BY C. LEWIS HIND
ADVENTURES AMONG PICTURES
24 FULL-PAGE ILLUSTRATIONS (8 IN COLOUR, 16 IN BLACK AND WHITE)

BY GERTRUDE DEMAIN HAMMOND
THE BEAUTIFUL BIRTH-DAY BOOK
12 FULL-PAGE ILLUSTRATIONS IN COLOUR
DECORATIVE BORDERS BY A. A. TURBAYNE

PAINTED BY JOHN FULLEYLOVE, R.I.
TEXT BY ROSALINE MASSON
EDINBURGH
21 FULL-PAGE ILLUSTRATIONS IN COLOUR

PAINTED BY GEORGE S. ELGOOD, R.I.
TEXT BY ALFRED AUSTIN, *Poet Laureate*
THE GARDEN THAT I LOVE
16 FULL-PAGE ILLUSTRATIONS IN COLOUR

BY LADY BUTLER
PAINTER OF "THE ROLL CALL"
LETTERS FROM THE HOLY LAND
16 FULL-PAGE ILLUSTRATIONS IN COLOUR BY LADY BUTLER

PAINTED AND DESCRIBED BY
MRS. WILLINGHAM RAWNSLEY
THE NEW FOREST
20 FULL-PAGE ILLUSTRATIONS IN COLOUR

PAINTED BY ARTHUR GEORGE BELL
DESCRIBED BY NANCY E. BELL
NUREMBERG
20 FULL-PAGE ILLUSTRATIONS IN COLOUR

PAINTED BY H. J. DOBSON, R.S.W.
DESCRIBED BY WM. SANDERSON
SCOTTISH LIFE AND CHARACTER
20 FULL-PAGE ILLUSTRATIONS IN COLOUR

PRINTED BY HELEN ALLINGHAM, R.W.S.
DESCRIBED BY ARTHUR H. PATERSON
THE HOMES OF TENNYSON
20 FULL-PAGE ILLUSTRATIONS IN COLOUR

BY W. EARL HODGSON
TROUT FISHING
WITH A MODEL BOOK OF FLIES IN COLOUR

BY C. LEWIS HIND
DAYS WITH VELASQUEZ
24 FULL-PAGE ILLUSTRATIONS (8 IN COLOUR AND 16 IN BLACK AND WHITE)

PAINTED BY JOHN FULLEYLOVE, R.I.
TEXT BY MRS. A. MURRAY SMITH
WESTMINSTER ABBEY
21 FULL-PAGE ILLUSTRATIONS IN COLOUR

BY OLIVER GOLDSMITH
THE VICAR OF WAKEFIELD
13 FULL-PAGE ILLUSTRATIONS IN COLOUR BY AN EIGHTEENTH-CENTURY ARTIST

BY GORDON HOME
YORKSHIRE
COAST AND MOORLAND SCENES
32 FULL-PAGE ILLUSTRATIONS IN COLOUR

PRICE 10s. NET EACH

PAINTED BY A. FORESTIER
DESCRIBED BY G. W. T. OMOND
BRUGES
AND WEST FLANDERS
33 FULL-PAGE ILLUSTRATIONS IN COLOUR

PAINTED BY NICO JUNGMAN
DESCRIBED BY G. E. MITTON
NORMANDY
40 FULL-PAGE ILLUSTRATIONS IN COLOUR

PUBLISHED BY A. & C. BLACK, SOHO SQUARE, LONDON, W.